Public Library
DeKalb, Illinois
RULES

1. Books may be retained for two weeks and may be renewed once for the same period unless otherwise indicated.

2. A fine is charged for each day that library material is overdue.

Young and Hungry

A Cookbook in the Form of a Memoir

Young and

1971

Hungry

A Cookbook in the Form of a Memoir

by SUZANNE TAYLOR

Illustrated by Mike Nelson

HOUGHTON MIFFLIN COMPANY, BOSTON

First printing c

Library of Congress Catalog Card Number: 74–120822
Printed in the United States of America

82191

For my granddaughters,
present and future

Preface

IN THE DINING ROOM of my house in Maine hangs an embroidery of gaily costumed people dancing; my Norwegian grandmother made this for me the Christmas I was five. By the raised brick fireplace in the living room stands a large copper kettle, somewhat battered through much use in years past, but always kept shining, and now usually used as a receptacle for garden flowers. It brings back to me memories of my grandmother's kitchen, redolent of good cooking smells. On the wall in my kitchen hangs a huge ornate copper pudding-mold, holding over ten quarts: my great-great-grandmother's; she had eleven children, so the size was appropriate.

On the far wall of the living room of the house in Maine hang miniatures of my great-great-great-grandfather, the awesome Bishop Primate of Norway, and his equally prim-looking wife and children. I feel far closer to the heritage of cooking than to the Bishopric, for I know him only by his portrait, whereas I spent much of my childhood in my Norwegian grandmother's kitchen. My Nordic heritage is all around me, and childhood habits still cling. I find myself murmuring "takk for maten" (thank you for the food) as I rise from the table, even if I have cooked the meal myself. And Christmas for me and my husband and children is always celebrated on

Christmas Eve, by their choice as well as mine. The heritage is strong.

A great part of our life is spent in our house on the coast of Maine, where earth and sea yield much the same provender as in Norway, so many of my grandmother's recipes have been adapted for use here. Although we do not have the variety of fresh fish available in those towns on the North Sea, we have the world's best lobster and succulent scallops and bright-eyed smelts, caught in winter through a hole in the ice. And in recent years the small Baltic shrimp has left its native waters and come to ours where it finds a hearty welcome. Where else in this age of inflation can you buy five pounds of fresh-caught shrimp for one slim dollar? You can in Maine.

Since my memories of childhood summers in Norway were for the most part happy ones, the customs of that country clung to me all through my childhood in Philadelphia. Our house had a foreign flavor, especially in the kitchen, and my school friends loved coming to our house and tasting the delicious things our Norwegian cook made. For a while the large brown goat's-milk cheese, sent out to us from Norway several times a year, disappeared so rapidly that my mother put a stop to the generous portions I cut off and gave to my demanding friends.

My childhood was quite different from that of my Philadelphia friends. For me there was no summer migration to the White Mountains of New Hampshire, or the south shore of Cape Cod. No pack trip in the Rockies, no summer camp with girls my own age. Instead, every year as soon as school ended (and sometimes before), our trunks were packed and Mother and I embarked on the sea trip to Norway, not to return until the day that my school began again.

My father's heritage was American, back to the colonial days of Virginia, but since he had no relatives living during my childhood, family life for me was epitomized by those large groups of relatives of my Norwegian mother who gathered around us during our summers in Norway.

I have gone back often over the years to my beloved Årdal. In spite of the fact that a short boat trip and a good road for cars has reduced that day-long trip of my childhood to under two hours, all else there seems unchanged. The river, still crystal clear, flows as swiftly over the rocks as when I used to jump from stone to stone; Sven, the farmer boy, now quite gray, still pastures his cows in the field nearby, and still sets his milk pails to cool in the deep pools.

Finnebu, our beloved fishing hut, has been cared for during the years by Cousin Astrid, who owns it and treasures it. The grass and flowers on the sod roof grow as luxuriantly as always, and the interior of the hut is still lit by the soft glow of candle-light and the kerosene lamps. Pollution has not yet reached that corner of the world. In my mind, it never can.

NOTE

A dagger marking the name of a dish or
dishes in the first four chapters indicates
that a corresponding recipe appears in
Chapter V.

The reader's good judgment will de-
termine how many persons may be served
by the quantities of ingredients specified
in each recipe.

Contents

Young and Hungry

A Cookbook in the Form of a Memoir

Stavanger

THE SEA GULLS had been our escort, following the white wake of the ship all the way across the North Sea on the last day of our journey. They floated majestically on their invisible cushion of air just above the after-rail of the ship. From time to time, losing their aloof dignity, they would dive down with piercing shrieks to retrieve the contents of a pail emptied out of the kitchen porthole far below, then rise again, resuming their positions in formation, wing-tip to wing-tip. Now small land birds came out to join them, darting and whirling among the gulls like a fleet of anxious tugboats, urging them on up the fjord to their destination.

Ahead of us the first islands, bare of any vegetation, and no larger than big rocks, rose from the morning-shiny blue sea. Then came a scattering of larger islands, some with patches of green grass and a few solitary sheep, that raised their heads from their browsing and emitted faint baa-aa's that floated out to us as the ship went by them. We were at the mouth of the Stavangerfjord, that deep cut of water piercing the rocky coast, identical, yet different from the thousands of others that bit into this rugged coast, all the way up to the northernmost cape. We passed a solitary white lighthouse. The Norwegian flag flew bravely at the peak of a flagpole beside it, and two small children stood on the rocky cliff waving to us. I always felt a small flip in the pit of my stomach at the first sight of that blue cross, outlined with white, on a red background. We were in Norway! More houses began to appear on the many islands, small wooden houses painted white, and while there were no trees on these windblown rocks, there was always a flagpole next to the house, with a flag gaily snapping in the breeze.

Mother was always up early for the "insailing." There were the usual goodbyes and exchange of addresses and there was usually some gentleman holding her hand in a reluctant farewell, but Mother would become impatient at this moment; the trip had been fun, and she might be happy to see these people again sometime on another crossing, or back in the United States, but right now she was anticipating picking up her Norwegian life again, renewing acquaintance with all those old friends who were undoubtedly at this moment planning parties to entertain her.

Mother had had a gay and carefree young life, and since she was the long-awaited daughter after six sons, and beautiful to boot, everything centered about her when she was young. She was a good skier and an excellent shot and handled a salmon rod well, having been thoroughly trained by her father and her brothers on many hunting and fishing expeditions to the lovely mountains of Norway. And with everything else there was a permanent officers' barracks just outside the city in those days. Mother danced her feet off, and broke hearts right and left.

She had gone to America when she was twenty-one, on a visit to one of her brothers in Philadelphia. There she met a handsome bachelor, already in his forties, who promptly fell in love with this young Nordic beauty. A few months after her visit ended, he pursued her back to Norway, proposed to her, and she accepted him.

On the whole, I think the marriage worked out well. Father was wise enough to know that he couldn't hold her if he didn't let her go home now and then to kick up her heels, and being a jealous man perhaps preferred to let her break loose all in one fell swoop where he couldn't see her and suffer by it. He did not care for the country life of hunting and fishing which made up a large part of our Norwegian summers, and on the rare occasions that he joined us there, he looked uneasy in his conservatively cut gray suits and his rather high, stiff collars. A city man, and wise enough to know it, he would suffer through a week in this bucolic atmosphere, and then was off to London and Paris to browse through museums and art galleries, before returning to his lonely house in America.

And so, every summer in early June, the big flat brown steamer trunks were packed, and my mother's equally large square hat trunk with her big hats securely pinned to the velvet-covered little cushions inside. The two plaid English blankets for our deck chairs were tightly rolled and secured by a leather carrying-strap, and all the trunks and heavy suitcases were sent on ahead from Philadelphia to the S.S. *Stavangerfjord,* or the *Bergensfjord,* sailing from Brooklyn a few days later.

My father accompanied Mother and me to the boat, and having seen us settled in our cabin, kissed us sadly goodbye, and went ashore. There were three loud blasts, and the gangplank was removed. As the water widened between dock and ship, I could see my father's small gray-clad figure give a final wave of his white handkerchief before he folded it and replaced it carefully in his breast pocket, points up, just so, and then turned away to start the lonely trip back to his empty house. I often wonder now what those long hot summers were like, with only the old housekeeper to look after him. I suppose he spent a

lot of time at his club. I would like to think he found someone
to console him during Mother's prolonged absence, but I have
a feeling that there was no one who could possibly have replaced her for him.

At lunch on Norwegian boats, there was a large table set up
in the center of the dining saloon, covered with dozens of plat-
ters of beautifully arranged cold food. This was the famous
Norwegian Koltbord, now universally known as Smørgåsbord.
You went and helped yourself to a plate from the stack at the
end of the table, and then, circling the table slowly and carefully you helped yourself first to the "fishy" things: herring
tidbits in dill sauce, tiny brisling sardines in oil, strong smoked
eel for the daring, fish salad decorated with cucumber and
radish for the less adventurous, and always, of course, the lovely
ubiquitous Norwegian smoked salmon, the best smoked salmon
in the world. (Scotsmen take notice!)

   I remember too, always on the Koltbord, a delicious salad of
† which the main ingredients were tuna fish and small white
beans. Evolving it out of memory, I make it often in summer
as a mainstay of our lunch. It keeps well for several days in the
refrigerator.

   After the fish dishes, back you went for a clean plate, and
piled it high with cold meats: Danish ham, a summer sausage
made of beef, a loaf of rolled spiced veal laced with parsley,
† and thinly sliced cold roast pork. At first I passed the cold roast
pork by, but when I saw the gentleman ahead of me help himself to three slices, I decided it must be good.

   Sometimes, as a special treat asked for by one of the Norwegian passengers, there would be a great steaming platter
brought up from the crew's kitchen, of that dish known to all
† seafaring men, Lapskaus (Lobscouse). We make it now just

as it is made on the Norwegian ships, in smaller proportions, and prettied up with lots of chopped parsley and a few peeled quarters of good ripe tomatoes nestling in a lettuce leaf at each end of the platter.

I suppose the sailors got tired of this oft-repeated dish as it was basic fare for them during the long months at sea, but for us it was a treat after all the fancy dishes we had been eating. And now my family find it a good filling dish after hours outdoors on a cold day.

Approaching Stavanger, the ship's engines were put in reverse, churning up a foam of white water all around us. It was a matter of pride for the Norwegian captains to dock their ships themselves without benefit of tugboats. They brought the large transatlantic steamer right up to the town dock as deftly and surely as though it were a small motorboat.

I spotted Grandfather's calèche, with the two brown horses, even before we were at the dock. And now I could see Carlson, the coachman, sitting up on the box, and Grandfather, who had got out of the carriage, and was standing beside it leaning slightly on his heavy gold-headed cane, and scanning the line of passengers at the rail of the docking ship, searching for his beloved daughter's face.

Although Stavanger was one of the larger cities of the country, in many ways it was still a small provincial town, and Mother's return from America every year, since she had been one of the town's reigning beauties, caused a stir.

"Bestefar," I shrieked, making myself heard above all the commotion going on on the dock. "Her er vi! Her er vi!" I switched happily from English to Norwegian at the first wave of the flag, and I usually managed to worm my way through the throng of people disembarking, and was one of the first off the boat. I threw myself upon my grandfather and flung my arms about his neck. "Bestefar, what has Bestemor got waiting for me this summer? A new cat?" My grandmother wisely reasoned that nothing attaches a solitary child as quickly as a house pet, so there was always some sort of small animal awaiting my arrival at my grandparents' house. Somehow the pets never seemed to survive from year to year, so there was a new one each time we came. My family said I loved them to death or just plain used them up. I still remember with horror the glazed expression in the eyes of the poor little white rabbit I accidentally ran over with my doll carriage. But I wasn't the only one. One summer, when I must have been very young as I barely remember it, there was a lamb named Lottie, who proved herself the proverbial follower, and must have become a nuisance to the grown-ups, for she suddenly disappeared in midsummer. It was not until years later that I connected the furry white rug that shortly afterwards appeared by my bed, with Lottie. By then, time, and a succession of other animals, had dimmed my memories of her, and I enjoyed the feeling of her furry sides under my bare feet without a qualm.

So now I begged Bestefar to tell me what enchanting animal might be mine, but he only looked mysterious, and told me to wait and see, as he returned my embrace.

Now Mother appeared at our side, and having embraced her, too, Grandfather held her at arm's length and looked her over to see if she had changed in the past year. Evidently what he saw pleased him, as he patted her on the shoulder and said, "Du Ellie" (his pet name for her), "du er akkurat den samme." And indeed she was unchanged, and as beautiful as when a young girl. Her straight back and magnificent carriage were inherited from her father. The heavy arching eyebrows that gave such emphasis to her blue eyes were also like his, but while hers were dark brown — much darker than her hair —

his eyebrows were now white. He still had his piercing blue eyes, but age had made them smaller, so that they almost disappeared under the bushy brows. I have seen pictures of him as a young man, and while all men at that time who wore the heavy, roundly-trimmed full-face beard and mustache bore a certain resemblance to one another, Grandfather so resembled pictures of the Czar of Russia at that epoch that his friends would joke with him about his "imperial look."

Now, Grandfather was white-haired, and the luxuriant dark beard had changed to a small, pointed white one, actually called an "imperial." He wore gold-rimmed spectacles, pince-nez, perched on the end of his fine straight nose, and always held his head high, and slightly tilted back, as though to keep the spectacles from sliding off the end. This also gave him the appearance of keeping the world at a certain distance.

We got into the calèche, leaving the luggage to follow later, but I insisted on carrying with me the box containing the top of the great cake from the Captain's Dinner of the night before, which the Captain himself had lifted off and given to me as the youngest member of the party. The top was all I could carry as the cake itself had stood almost three feet high.

That magnificent product of the pastry chef's art, called the Kransekake, or Pyramid Cake, is a cake for special occasions. † Crunchy baked rings of almond-flavored cake, starting with the largest ring as a base, are piled carefully on top of each other, each one slightly smaller than the one below, the whole forming a towering pyramid, and the entire cake decorated with a zigzag tracery of white icing. But that is only the beginning. Then flags and favors, candies and snappers, anything and everything appropriate to the occasion, are stuck all over it, held in place with caramelized sugar, and on the top — O crowning glory! — a miniature ship, all sails set, made entirely of spun sugar, and surrounded by many small Norwegian and American flags.

As we drove away from the dock, Mother and Grandfather caught up with each other's news, while I looked with renewed joy at all the familiar places. We drove past the cobblestoned marketplace, where the stalls were bright with early vegetables and the first strawberries, too red to have ripened here this early, so perhaps sent on from Holland along with the nodding, brightly colored tulips. Up the winding narrow hill, past the pastry shop where I often went to stuff myself when Grandfather gave me an extra krone to spend, and then turning left into the wide street where the houses were larger, and set back in neat gardens with graveled paths winding among the flower beds.

My grandparents' house was at the end of the street. It was a wooden house of the Victorian period, painted a pale yellow with brown trim. It was quite tall, with three stories, and an attic on top, making it a little too high for its width, so that the third floor, with its crenelated balconies and gingerbread trim under the roof, gave it the appearance of a tall lady with a large fussy hat on her head. Mother's parents were fairly prosperous, and while their standard of living was not lavish for those days (except where food was concerned), there were always three maids in the house and a coachman to drive Grandmother on her errands and visits.

As we drove up, Grandmother would be just behind the large front gate, bending over a potted fuchsia plant, pretending that she was occupied with gardening rather than anxiously awaiting our arrival. And what was that perched on the fence post beside her? I was out of the carriage in a flash and caught up the fluffy white kitten with a blue bow around its neck, and I hope that Bestemor understood that the enthusiastic display of affection that it received from me was also intended for her.

Grandmother was small and plump and pretty, with tiny hands and feet. She rarely walked outside her house and garden. She was quicker and sharper and wittier than Mother and Grandfather, who resembled each other. She was a magnificent housekeeper and loved to entertain. I think she got a vicarious pleasure out of her daughter's social engagements, and I'm sure she primed all her friends for Mother's arrival. On entering the front hall we found the silver tray on the side table overflowing with cards and invitations.

So we settled into the life of Stavanger, as spring turned to summer, and the days grew long and light and lovely.

Every day, at a few minutes before two, Grandfather came walking up the long hill from downtown, where he had been to the Bourse to look at the latest stock quotations. He opened the small gate at the bottom of the garden, and as he moved up the path he stopped to look at each rose on his tall-stemmed tree roses. The white Snow Queen always got an extra minute or two, for this was truly the queen of the garden, and while its blossoms were never as profuse as were the velvety red roses, or the little pink mossy ones, the Snow Queen's blooms were so large, each creamy white petal perfectly formed, and they gave off such a delicious delicate perfume that it seemed she really had a right to hold her head a bit higher than her more prolific sisters.

As the sound of Grandfather's boots crunching on the gravel path was heard in the house, the bustle in the kitchen increased in tempo. Sigrid, the waitress, rushed into the dining room, placing on the table those last-minute things: the cut-crystal dish with thin-shaven butterballs, painstakingly made with a little curved metal blade; the carafe of homemade fruit syrup at my place, with a small pitcher of cold water to dilute it; at Grandfather's place a tall tapering glass with his initials, MW, engraved on it in Gothic script, next to a newly opened bottle of Danish beer, and then the oval bread basket with five kinds of bread. There was "Groftbrød" (pumpernickel) for Grandfather, Kristiania brød (a seedless rye) for Grandmother, and Fransk brød, a special home-baked bread made with the finest white flour, for my mother, who, having lived away a number of years, was no longer accustomed to the good coarse breads of her native land. There was also a sweet spicy raisin bread, and Flatbrød, a kind of paper-thin Ry-Krisp. I ate it all.

On the sideboard stood the big silver coffee tray, set for after-dinner coffee, with the thin gold-and-white Limoges coffee cups, and the gold-and-enamel coffee spoons. There was a sort of ritual about the spoons: you tried to match the color of the beautiful enameled handles to the dress or the personalities of those who were to use them. If there was a guest you disliked, you contrived to give him the poison green. Grandfather always had the dark velvety red one, Bestemor had lavender, and Mother's color was a blue to match her eyes. It was a color she wore a great deal. The bright yellow one was mine. I was particularly fond of it as the enamel handle was cracked and there was a distinct tooth-mark in the bowl of it, made by my Uncle Thomas when he was my age. Somehow it brought that tall, rather awesome man down to my level.

On the coffee tray there was also a squat silver cream pitcher, for the thick cream that had been brought to a boil and then let cool in the larder, so that great clots came to the surface. I discovered years later that it was exactly like England's Devonshire cream. Grandmother spooned a large dollop into each cup when she served the coffee. But the thing I loved best on the tray was the big sugar bowl, filled with crystallized sugar, and covered by a small square of fine net to keep off the flies. The net had a border of small conical seashells to weigh it down around the sugar bowl, and it had been sent from South Africa by my Uncle Thomas, the one of Mother's six brothers who had gone off to Capetown to seek his fortune. I knew every one of the seashells by heart, and found it a never-ending source of wonder that those shells, gathered on such a distant beach, were there in our dining room in Norway. The fact that I had traveled four thousand miles to find myself in this same dining room was no source of wonder to me at all.

Uncle Thomas and his English wife rarely took the long boat trip from Capetown to spend a summer here in the North, but when they did, it was a time of great excitement for me. Uncle Thomas was tall and lean, with the regular features of all the family, but he had a more deeply-lined and brown face than the others, I suppose from all those years spent under the hot African sun. He had marvelous stories to tell, this African uncle — stories of the Matabele, a Zulu tribe that lived deep in the jungle and once danced a war dance beneath him while he hid all night high in a tree; of giant ants that had been known to trap an unwary child when she stepped on their nest, and eat her alive in two minutes flat, leaving a small heap of clean-picked bones.

The other thing that tied me to Uncle Thomas was our common love of desserts. When Bestemor tired of hearing me cry, "What-are-we-having-for-dessert-today?" and scolded me for it, I could always get Uncle Thomas to ask in my place. It was an all-important question to me, because I carefully gauged the amount I would eat of the main course, according to what was to come at the end of the meal. If it was Lemon or Pineapple †
Fromage, I held back on the meat and the vegetables. If it was †
to be a Rum Omelet, a dessert my elders were partial to, but †

not one of my favorites, I would eat the meat and vegetables dutifully without too much urging. I found the Rum Omelet beautiful to look at, its soft brown crust gently containing the foamy insides, and the whole surface sprinkled with confectioners' sugar; and the first spoonful, airy and light, was delicious, but I didn't care for the taste it left in my mouth, nor for the smell of it. It reminded me of Dagfinn, Grandfather's secretary, who sometimes smelled that way.

Dagfinn, a tall, blond, weedy young man, stood all day at the big high desk in Grandfather's office on the third floor of the house, filling page after page in the account book with his tenuous, slanted handwriting. I felt sorry for him . . . all that work to be done indoors in nice summer weather. Sometimes he would come down into the living room while we were having coffee after dinner, with papers for Grandfather to sign. He always managed to go and stand quite close to Mother, and say How do you do to her in a tense, low voice. Mother didn't seem to care for him at all, and either ignored him completely, or was very short with him and moved away.

I, on the other hand, thought him rather fascinating with his high, flat cheekbones, and thick blond lashes fringing gray green eyes that had an upward slant at the outer corners, giving him a strange Norse-Oriental look.

One day, as I stood by his desk watching him making more ink blotches on the pages than usual, I got a whiff of something that made me wonder if he had been down to our kitchen. He smelled very strongly of Rum Omelet. I was standing quite close to him, trying to peer around him at the account book and see how many mistakes he had made.

"Oh, poor Dagfinn," I said. "Grandfather will be furious at you when he sees this page. Let me see if I can't get rid of that big ink splotch in the middle for you."

I was leaning across him, trying to catch the edge of the still wet splotch with a corner of the blotter I held, when some sixth sense made me straighten up and draw back a little. What a funny watery look his eyes had, and when he put his hand on my shoulder, which he sometimes did in a friendly way, it felt . . . different, and to my amazement the hand started to move slowly and caressingly down over the front of my pink angora sweater. Suddenly feeling hot and prickly all over, I stood rooted to the spot, too embarrassed to utter a word, and vainly trying to draw in my budding bosom.

"Søte lille Tutti," he mumbled, which also startled me slightly as this was the pet name only my family used. "You're going to give that proud bitch downstairs a run for her money one of these days." With which he leaned over and planted a big wet kiss on my innocent mouth. This was altogether too much for me, and terribly confused at his words, as well as his actions, I turned and bolted and ran out of the room, bumping into Grandfather in the doorway, down three flights of stairs and into the lavatory, where I locked the door and promptly burst into tears. As I fled I heard loud voices from the top of the house, and five minutes later more footsteps came pounding down the stairs. The front door slammed, and that was the last I saw of Dagfinn.

I loved Grandfather's office. It was a big square room on the third floor of the house. The predominating color was brown, and the atmosphere was slightly musty. All around the room, reaching almost to the high ceiling, were glass-doored cabinets, with shelves displaying row upon row of rather dusty small glass jars, with fat cork stoppers, holding samples of the various syrups he imported from South America and Cuba. Sometimes I would pry a stopper out carefully, and stick my finger in for a

taste. Some of the syrups were dark brown, very thick, and had a sort of burnt taste, while others were pale yellow and merely sweet. Once in a while, if we were having pancakes for dessert,
† especially the little ones made from leftover rice, Grandmother would say it was a great pity to have all those syrups up there going to waste, and could she please have something to pour on the pancakes. Grandfather would take quite some time deciding which of his precious samples he could spare, and would bring the little jars down to the kitchen, handing them over reluctantly to Grandmother, rather as though he were being asked to cash in some of his stocks and bonds.

† Karen, the cook, also made lovely thin little pancakes to be rolled up with a filling of jelly, and dusted with confectioners' sugar. It was a special treat for me when she used my favorite jelly made from a mixture of raspberries and red currants.

Recipes for fruit jellies are found in every standard cookbook, so I am not going to repeat them here, but I will tell you of a trick I learned from Karen, who made jellies before the days of commercial pectin. If I am using a fruit that has little natural pectin in it, I cut up one or two underripe apples and boil them with my fruit as she did. This should add enough natural pectin to the juice of raspberries or grapes or currants to assure you of their jelling, and it does not affect the taste.

† There were blueberry pancakes too, made from the small, full-flavored berries that grow wild in Norway, and are so abundant here in our own state of Maine.

† There was a hot Fruit Soup that Karen made in summer from a succession of fruits and berries. This was one of Grandfather's favorites, and I liked it more than I would admit, since I was always being told that it was *good* for me. The strange thing is that while I distinctly recall the deep white porcelain soup plates with the blue and gold border, I cannot remember if we

ate it as a first or last course. A dish rarely served here, it has been common in northern Europe since the fourteenth century, and is still a popular dish in Germanic countries. I think its popularity might be more universal if it were served hot, at the end of a cold summer lunch or dinner.

Very often (not often enough for me) we had Krumkaker, † thin crisp round wafers, made in a special flat baking iron, something like a small waffle iron with a flowery embossed design that imprinted itself on the wafer. This was taken out of the iron when baked to a delicate brown, and quickly popped into a cup while still warm, to cool and harden into the shape of the cup. It was fun to do — you had to be ever so quick — and I loved helping. And there were so many ways to serve Krumkaker: we filled them with whipped cream and raspberries, or strawberries, or sometimes with Mocha-Chocolate † Mousse, a delectable blend of crisp cake and cool sweet contents. In this, as in many good desserts, the contrast in texture counts as much as the flavor.

On Sundays dinner was not until three o'clock. In the morning Grandmother and I would go off to church, leaving Grandfather to putter in the garden among his roses. Mother had usually been out late the night before, at a dinner or a ball, and since her parents loved to know that she was enjoying herself, she was allowed to sleep late.

So Mother was excused from church, but Bestemor and I went every Sunday. Carlson was always outside with the calèche long before it was time to go, and seemed to take particular pleasure in showing the neighbors how anxious he and his horses were to get to church, even if we weren't. There was a great deal of yelling and pulling on the reins, which only served to excite the horses still more, so that by the time Grandmother had gathered together her prayer book, her gloves, and her purple beaded bag with the little bottle of smelling salts in it, and came out the front door, the horses were prancing as though they were off to the races. Carlson was apparently of the same mind, and would start off down the cobblestone hill at a rush, with Grandmother poking him in the back with her little black parasol, trying to make him slow down, trying to make herself heard above all the clatter. "Carlson, you simply must control the horses or Wallem (she called my grandfather by his last name, even when addressing him) will have to find a coachman for me who can!" Nevertheless, Carlson lasted long enough to graduate to an automobile which he drove in the same mad fashion, wrestling with the steering wheel as he had with the reins, and talking to the car with the same excited urgency with which he formerly addressed his horses.

We would arrive at the great twelfth-century stone cathedral in time for Grandmother to greet two or three friends as we started up the broad steps, with me bobbing a succession of small curtsies — obligatory in Norway for any well-brought-up girl until she was eighteen and suddenly considered an adult.

I followed Grandmother's rustling purple silk down the aisle, and slid into the pew after her as the minister, with his great white pleated ruff topping his black robes, began the Lutheran service. Grandmother timed it just so. As soon as we were seated we bowed our heads and said a silent prayer. Grandmother always remained with bowed head for several minutes, which bothered me as I thought it rude somehow for us to be saying our own private prayers, while the minister had already begun his communal prayer for all of us. How confusing for God!

The church was enormous, and the minister so far away up there in his high, ornately carved and painted pulpit that his words rarely disturbed my daydreams, and I only came to when the hymns started, and I had to decipher the queer old-fashioned Gothic Norwegian script in the Hymnal. No one sang very loudly except the minister, who seemed bent on waking anyone careless enough to have fallen asleep while he was speaking. Unfortunately he lacked both sense of tempo and pitch, and I, who loved to sing, would lift up my voice as loudly as possible, hoping in this way to get the rest of the congregation to follow *me,* not *him.* But it was of no use, for after a few verses of this, people in the pews ahead of us would turn and stare, Grandmother would put her hand firmly over mine and say, "Tutti, da! Ti stille!" and I would give up and wander musically astray with the rest of them.

As we walked out at the end of the service, Grandmother would sigh happily and say, "You should have seen your mother on her wedding day here in this cathedral! She was the most beautiful bride the town had ever seen, and besides all the people in the church, there were hundreds lined up outside on the square to catch a glimpse of her when she came out on the arm of the handsome American who was going to take her so far away. And your poor dear father . . . married in a language he did not understand one word of! Dear man."

Sometimes after church we went to the cemetery to see that the Wallem plot was being properly cared for. It was a lovely cemetery, with large trees shading it, and the neat gravel-paved plots, surrounded by flowers, looked like miniature well-laid-out parks. Some of them had a white-painted iron chair next to the tombstone — invitation to linger. It all looked very gentle and uncrowded. Once Grandmother pointed out a little old woman dressed in a long gray skirt and a matching jacket of old-fashioned cut. She was scurrying about among the plots, talking to herself in a scolding way. "There goes poor old Miss Opsfelder," said Grandmother. "She spends her days wandering through the cemetery inspecting the graves. If she thinks a plot is not well taken care of, she jots down the name on the tombstone, and whether she knows the family or not, looks up their address and writes the living members a scathing letter telling them that it is a shame and a sin to neglect their dead so." And Grandmother nodded approvingly.

By the time we got home, preparations for dinner were well under way, and usually the lovely smell of roast lamb was wafted toward us as we came up the garden path. Our leg of † lamb was prepared in a special way before roasting. Little slits or pockets were cut into it, and these were stuffed with freshly chopped parsley. When carved and served, each slice would have a round patch of parsley, looking pretty and giving the meat a delicious flavor.

Or we would have a dish that was very special to Bestemor's † house, Benløse Fugler, which translates as Boneless Birds, but has nothing to do with veal birds as we make them. Or we † might have Surstek, a kind of marinated pot roast.

While there was not a great variety of vegetables in Norway, such as we are used to now in the United States, the vegetables that we did get were always deliciously fresh. They were probably picked in some garden only a few miles outside town, and brought in to be sold the same day in the big open-air marketplace, and appeared on our table that evening. There were big solid heads of cabbage, tender small carrots, beautiful creamy-white heads of cauliflower, tiny peas, and a kind of pea that you ate, pod and all. There they were called Sukkererter, Sugar † Peas, but they are called Mange-Tout in France, and Snow Peas by the Chinese, who use them in many of their dishes. They are delicate to the taste, but easy to grow, and since they are eaten pod and all, there is not that endless shelling to do.

All the vegetables were used in a variety of ways, and one of

my favorite supper dishes was Cauliflower with Shrimps — a †
whole head of fresh boiled cauliflower, adorned with little pink
shrimps in a light cream sauce. Or Stuffed Head of Cabbage: a †
whole head of cabbage would be scooped out, filled with a delicious meat stuffing, and served with a thin cream sauce.

Sunday dessert was sure to be something special like Riskrem
med Rød Saus (Almond Rice Pudding with Fruit Sauce). †
Or meringues! If there were three or four egg whites left over
from custards, or a sauce demanding yolks for thickening,
Karen made meringues for dessert. Sometimes small individual †
ones with crushed berries poured over, and at other times she
made them into two large round layers, held together with
chocolate-flavored whipped cream.

The strawberries and raspberries in Norway seemed the best
in the world! The summer season was short, but the days were
so long that there was almost continual sun around the clock
to make up for it, and the fruit ripened steadily, growing larger
and sweeter than any I have tasted since. In the garden, off at
one end, was a great tangle of raspberry bushes. The stone wall
behind sheltered them from wind, and held every last bit of
warmth from the sun. I was taught to pick the juicy red berries
carefully without squashing them, and as a reward for filling
the berry pail, Grandfather would say, "Let's see if there are
any of the white ones this year." They really weren't white at
all, but a lovely pale translucent yellow, and slightly larger than
the red raspberries, though they grew on two spindly bushes,
hard to find among the more robust red ones. I would select a
large plump pale berry, and crushing it slowly with my tongue
against the roof of my mouth, let the sweet juice trickle down
my throat. Undoubtedly the staple fare of the gods!

In another corner of the garden were the gooseberry bushes,

and when I arrived, early in the summer, I would rush down to see if any of the gooseberries were ripe. They were not supposed to be ripe for another month, but I would go hopefully to the garden each day, squeezing one or two of the hard berries to see if there was any change. Since Nature, when left to herself, is in no particular hurry, my patience was sorely tried.

As they ripened, the small round pink ones with rather whiskery skins turned rosy-red, the pale greeny-yellow ones became exactly the right shade of deep, buttery yellow, and the big, smooth, oval green ones grew larger and shinier until you knew the moment had come, and popped one into your mouth, where it burst like a small balloon, filling your mouth with its sweet jellylike contents. The gooseberries were made into a delicious

† dessert with a very long name, Stikkelsbaergrøt. This was one of the everyday desserts — not a party dish at all, but one of my favorites — just the berries cooked with some sugar, and slightly thickened. Raspberries and cherries, and later in the season, plums were all cooked in much the same way.

A great many preserves were made as the fruit ripened in the garden, for Grandmother could not bear to see anything go to waste. There was raspberry jam, but mostly — because Grandfather didn't like the seeds — the raspberries were combined with red currants to make a delectable jelly. And black currants, "sunberries," mixed with the red, were made into a heavy wine-red jelly, very good to eat with game.

Most European schools have a much briefer summer vacation than we do in the United States. Consequently, when I arrived in Stavanger, the other children were still at their lessons. By the time their vacations began, and I had someone to play with, my grandparents and Mother would whisk me off to our place in the mountains, where they liked to spend most of the summer salmon-fishing and entertaining visitors. In those days people didn't worry very much about children lacking companions of their own age.

In Stavanger the garden was my kingdom. In a way, it was my prison too, but I didn't mind. Such a lovely prison. On rare occasions a child would be found to come play with me for an afternoon, usually the granddaughter of friends of my grandparents. She would arrive all done up in starched white dress and white shoes, which immediately precluded such pastimes as tree climbing, and I'm sure she loathed me as much as I loathed her. We didn't even have the benefit of a language barrier, since I could speak Norwegian. We were of course forbidden to leave the garden, and for diversion, around teatime, we were each given a cup and a spoon, and an egg yolk. A bowl of sugar was set between us, and we were allowed to make Eggedosis. This was a somewhat sickly sweet concoction, † but it served several purposes: it gave us the opportunity to make something we could eat, it kept us in one spot, not necessarily bothering the cook in the kitchen, and it solved the problem of entertainment for an hour. The idea was that you stirred and stirred the egg yolk, gradually adding small amounts of sugar, until the whole mass became very smooth and almost white. This took concentration and a certain amount of time. The only trouble was that we never could resist the temptation to taste as we went along, so that by the time it reached the desired consistency there was very little left in the bottom of the cup. It was essentially a children's party dish, but the grown-ups also indulged sometimes, if they were sitting around the garden on a summer afternoon. They always added a good dollop of brandy, "to cut the sweetness." I use it now in a slightly modified form as a sauce for stewed peaches or pears, and it is delicious poured over blackberries or blueberries.

While I did not care for the few carefully selected little girls
of my grandmother's choice, I did have one friend who lived
just down the hill — my one and only "best friend." She was
almost two years older than I, very pretty, and allowed much
more freedom than I was. All this lent her added glamour in
my eyes, but alas, Grandmother did not approve either of
Thelma's background or of her upbringing, and my friendship
with her was definitely frowned upon. Thelma lived alone
with her mother, who seemed to be a perfectly nice, normally
pretty young woman. But my grandmother's word for her was
"frivolous," and the way Grandmother used it, it was a very
strong word indeed! Thelma's father was a sea captain in the
Australian trade, and only came home for a month's leave,
every two or three years. I suppose Thelma's pretty mother
consoled herself as best she could for this somewhat desultory
marriage. I was only permitted to see Thelma once or twice a
week at most, and was never allowed to go with her and her
harum-scarum companions to the town bathing beach, or take
a picnic up in the hills with them. I would watch wistfully
from our garden as they all went off on their bicycles, a gay
laughing group.

Sometimes they would be playing in the street nearby when
suddenly the air would tremble with the sound of three great
blasts from a ship's siren, and they would all drop whatever they
were doing, and go tearing pell-mell down the hill, shouting
"Amerika båten! Amerika båten!" It was the monthly transatlantic steamer from America coming up the fjord. I sometimes managed to get away with the group on these occasions,
and we all arrived panting, on the dock, just as the boat was
inching in to the pier. For some reason the big ship impressed
me much more as I stood on the dock with my companions
looking up at it than when I was a passenger on it. And then

I had a private feeling, all my own. It had been to my homeland, America, since I last saw it, and I was the only one of the group who understood what that meant.

One summer, a few years after the First World War, "the gang" of boys and girls was suddenly swelled by visiting children called "Vienerkind." They were German children, suffering from the ravages of war in their country, and the kindly Norwegians had taken them into their homes for the summer months, to rehabilitate them. I particularly recall a dark, hollow-eyed, close-cropped, sharp-featured boy named Kurt, who would leave the group playing ball in the street, and dart into our kitchen. He would cram both mouth and pockets full of whatever Karen offered him, and thus provisioned against his insatiable hunger, return to the game.

It wasn't many years later, in 1939, that I heard that Kurt was back in Stavanger with others of the Vienerkind, all resplendent in Nazi uniform, to take over the city that had cared for them.

In spite of my family, Thelma and I would meet by prearranged signal, usually up in the lofty branches of a big maple tree at the foot of our garden. There we would sit for hours, on a rather precarious little platform we had rigged up, drinking lemon soda pop, and talking about all those things girls that age do talk about. Thelma was a fund of slightly garbled knowledge about many things, and her contributions to the conversation were a constant revelation to me. The day she told me "the Facts of Life" in very basic terms, shorn of all the romantic embellishments I had been brought up on by my fond mother, I dropped my pop bottle and almost fell out of the tree.

On one of the rare occasions when I was allowed to stay and have dinner with Thelma and her mother, we had a dish I had

† never eaten before. I was asked if I liked Fårikål, a lamb and cabbage stew, to which I politely replied, "Yes, but not too much cabbage, please." I understood their slightly baffled expressions later, when I saw that the stew was as much cabbage as meat. I have revised it a bit for my own use, and added a greater proportion of meat, since I have a family of men, and they all like it.

Since I was alone so much of the time, I had plenty of opportunity to read, but there were not many books in English in my grandparents' house, and when you are wolfing books as fast as you can, you want to read them in your own language. Fortunately for me Uncle Petter, a bachelor cousin of Mother's, lived only a short walk away from us. He had been a sea captain in the Orient, spoke English and French and Mandarin Chinese, and had a large bookcase crammed full of assorted volumes. A good half of them were in English, the popular and much-traveled Tauchnitz paperbacks. I was allowed to borrow two books at a time, and loved to go and fetch them from his small white clapboard house, which was as neat and tidy as ship's quarters. A great shiny brass ship's bell hung outside the front door, the windowsills were crowded with a profusion of flowers in bloom in an assortment of different-sized pots, and the hearth in the cozy living room was nicely cluttered with highly polished copper pots and kettles. All this was kept shining and clean and blooming by Bina, his housekeeper-cook. She used to stand watching me indulgently as I ran to the glass-doored cabinet that held mementos of Uncle Petter's years in the Orient, and tried on the Japanese clogs, wound the green- and gold-embroidered obi around my fat middle, and picked up the jangling Javanese bracelets.

"Where did Uncle Petter get these?" I would ask Bina.

"Off one of those foreign dancing girls, no doubt," she would reply with a slight sniff. Reluctantly I replaced the treasures in the cabinet, as Bina went off to the kitchen to get me a piece of her just-baked Apple Cake. Although I came for books, † I came for the Apple Cake too. My appetite went in many directions.

Uncle Petter's reading tastes were certainly varied, and for a preteen girl some of the books were pretty heavy going, while others would surely have been censored by my family, had they bothered to look. I consumed a dog-eared copy of something I think was titled *Lucy's First Affair,* and well-worn copies of *Confessions of a Chambermaid* and *In an Oriental Harem.*

But then, being young and hungry, I devoured with equal fervor Boswell's *Life of Johnson,* and found it equally fascinating, and breezed happily through *The Mill on the Floss,* with only a slight headache to show for it. I had all of Jack London, and all of Joseph Conrad. I worked my way through huge volumes of Dickens, and then found, to my frustration, that *Nicholas Nickleby* was in Danish. I only hesitated for a moment, however, and then ate my way through that. I don't remember how many times I read *Tess of the d'Urbervilles,* but I do remember that I shed tears over it year after year.

I think the most fortunate aspect of this summer reading program was that no one edited, no one forbade, no one imposed a book. I read them all: dull, indifferent, and exciting. They were my hidden secret treasure trove that I rediscovered every summer.

Grandfather had wonderful ways of entertaining me, and having had seven children of his own, was quite at ease with me. One of my first memories is of the big gold pocket-watch he carried, and which he hung at night on a hook on the wall

beside his bed, against a small round piece of green flannel
embroidered with a garland of pink roses, to ward off the chill.
It seemed wrong to him, and to all men of that time (at least,
in Norway) to take a watch that had been in a warm pocket all
day, and hang it bare and unprotected against a cold wall.

Whenever I wanted to open the back of the watch to see
what was inside, Grandfather would say, "No, then the fly
that lives in there will escape, and the watch will run down,"
and for years my belief in the legendary fly kept me from ever
trying to open it. He made wonderful little whistles for me
out of hollow sticks, and taught me how to blow an ear-split-
ting blast on a tightly held blade of grass, and he made the best
bows and arrows that anyone ever had.

He used to take me with him to the open marketplace down
on the town square. The large square was really the center
of town, although most of the good shops were down a winding
street a few blocks away. At the upper end of the square
stood the huge stone cathedral, backed by a park and a large
pond inhabited by black swans with gaudy red beaks. The
square was separated from all this by a wide street, marked
by the statue of the town's most famous author, who managed
to look important in spite of the sea gulls that landed on his
head, and left their mark all over his shoulders. The square
sloped on down to the harbor where all the boats came in, large
liners as well as the small fishing boats that went out the fjord
to the North Sea every day. The day's catch was displayed
and sold from big wooden tables set up on the cobblestones
right at the water's edge. In this way the fishermen could reach
back for more supplies from the boats bobbing at their moorings
directly behind them.

It would never have entered Grandfather's head to do any of
the other marketing — that was women's work — but when it

came to selecting a fine fish, they relied on his practiced eye.
In a coastal town no one would think of buying a fish that
wasn't alive, but for Grandfather it had to be so lively it was
practically jumping off the table. There were codfish and
flounder, halibut and hake, rosy pink salmon, and, considered
best of all, the pale pink Sea Trout. There were crabs and North †
Sea lobsters and big baskets of pink bristly shrimps. There
were small fresh herring that Karen used in pancakes (yes, †
pancakes!) for supper, and for one short month, the beautiful
pink crayfish, halfway in size between lobster and shrimp, so ·
delicate, so delicious, and so difficult to open.

Having made his selection after a great deal of poking and
prodding to see if the flesh was good and firm, Grandfather
had the fish quickly dispatched, cleaned, wrapped in a sheet
of newspaper, and into our basket it went, to be hurried home
to Karen in the kitchen.

Sometimes fish was bought for a Fish and Vegetable Chow- †
der, served up in the big blue-and-white Canton china tureen,
with a sprinkling of finely chopped chive to garnish it, a meal
in itself. If we had bought a piece of halibut, or any large fish
to be served whole, there was sure·to be enough to make Fiske †
Kreteng the following day. A great many French cooking
terms were adapted to Norwegian use, and Fiske Kreteng no
doubt started out as Fisk au Gratin, just as the Norwegian
Vullevang began as Vol-au-vent.

Grandfather was the center of the household to me, and what
I loved most was the rare evening when, having tapped the big
barometer that hung on the dining-room wall by the door, he
would turn to me and say, "It looks as though it would be a
fine day tomorrow. Would you like to go and see the lark
rise?"

The lark was a very early riser, and at 4:00 A.M. Grandfather and I were already on our way, walking the dusty road out of town to Våland, a small rise in the midst of flat green wheat fields, topped by an old stone watchtower. Grandfather, in his rough brown tweeds, old felt hat, walking stick in one hand, holding on to me with the other, walked along, head thrown back in order to look through the spectacles that sat at the end of his fine straight nose, and warned me not to make a sound. Arrived at a certain point on the road, he would say, "Now you must stand absolutely still. The lark is a very shy little bird and we mustn't frighten her. Just keep looking at this field on our left."

One . . . two . . . three minutes passed. It was quite light by now, although the daisies and bluebells still dripped dewy heads. Faint sounds, and a thin trail of rising smoke from some farm in the distance: the world was just waking up.

Suddenly, as though a spring had been released, there was a movement in the grass, almost at our feet. A little bird darted up, singing the most joyful song — a veritable paean to the sun, up, up, straight up, until I could hardly see him against the blue, but his jubilant song still came down to us, and as he soared another bird would start up, a third, and a fourth, from different parts of the field, straight up as though pulled by invisible strings, trilling away, an improvised heavenly chorus.

So sure was his course, so triumphant his song that as I stood there, brown-sandaled feet firmly planted in the dusty road, head thrown way back, watching the distant speck, I suddenly felt that he was taking me along, and I danced on wings up there with him.

It was all over in a matter of minutes, and Grandfather and I turned and walked silently home to the breakfast of hot rolls and café au lait awaiting us. In spite of the sixty years' differ-

ence that lay between us, I think the feeling we had was
exactly the same: that we had just witnessed something wonderful, almost like the creation of the world, and that there was no
need to try to discuss it either with each other, or with anyone
else.

Finnebu

It was already past the first of July — salmon-fishing time — and preparations to leave for Årdal were in full swing. Årdal — my Årdal (pronounced as though spelled oardoll) was a small country village, deep in the Ryfylke Fjord, and not the larger commercial town by the same name that is better known. It was one of hundreds of isolated villages that dot the country, and had a fine, beautiful river that began high up in the mountains.

Now suitcases were brought down from the attic and cluttered the bedrooms; tins of English biscuits and marmalades and cheeses — all the things we couldn't buy in the country — arrived from Leverson's Grocery Store, piled up on every available counter in the kitchen so poor Karen hardly had room to move. Smoked sausages were brought out from the place where they hung in the larder, jars of preserves, especially the precious Tyttebaer (lingonberries) were carefully wrapped in news- † paper, and packed in a big carton marked "Forsiktigbehandling" (handle with care). Cases of beer and wine would be delivered to the boat, for Årdal was a dry village. And all Grandfather's flat tin boxes of beautiful feathery salmon-flies were opened, their contents carefully gone over to see what was missing, what delectable tidbit would be needed this year to lure the wary fish. Fortunately the fishing rods were left in the hytte from summer to summer, so we didn't have to cope with those too.

When I went back to Årdal a few years ago, I found it was possible to reach the hut in an hour and a half from Stavanger, door to door, but in my childhood it was a matter of a long boat trip, followed by a long carriage ride. We said it "spoiled the better part of a day." There was a choice of three boats, all of which made five or six stops before reaching our destination at the very end of the fjord. If we were lucky enough to be leaving on a day that the *Hjelmeland* was going, the trip was off to a good start, for this boat was relatively new, and only took four hours to reach Årdal, instead of the five or six hours the other two rolling little tubs took. These boats were built basically for short day trips, and the only place to sit indoors was the smoking room. Since this was apt to be stuffy and crowded, we usually sat on the deck on small folding stools, or walked about, as it took really bad weather to drive us indoors. The two setters, Rick and Nelly, being well-trained hunting dogs, lay quietly at Grandfather's feet.

The monotony of the long trip was broken by the stops at small villages on the way. The little steamer would give a short blast of her horn, and we could see people come running down to the dock as we eased our way in to let off passengers, mail, and city orders from the summer people staying there. We would take on baskets of fruit and vegetables, and big metal milk cans, all to be brought to the city on the return trip that evening. Sometimes a few pigs, pushed unwillingly up the gangplank, or a cow, going to some farm further along our route, would join us.

Now, finally, the rope was cast off from the last village before ours. Already around the bend I could see the top of the moun-

tain that marked Årdal village. It was distinctive among all the
surrounding mountains, for way up on its rocky southern slope
was a small patch of bright green grass, planted by an enterprising farmer who pastured his cows there in summer. To me
it was a banner — a flag greeting me, telling me I was home.

The village below, with its thirty or forty wooden houses,
most of them painted white, with a few yellow or red ones here
and there, lay before us at the very end of the long narrow
fjord. At this moment an open motor launch usually came
zipping along, headed in the same direction, and obviously
trying to beat us in. This was the boat run by the Farmers'
Syndicate, between their village and the city. Leaving Stavanger at the same time that we did, but being a much smaller
boat, it took about the same number of hours to run straight
back as we did with all our stops. If it managed to reach the
dock before us, there would be a shout of triumph from the
farmers. I don't know what the rules and regulations about
that boat were; none of us ever set foot on it. I don't know if
it was a matter of snobbery, and if so, on whose part, although
the line between city folk and peasants was very clearly drawn
— even the language was different — but perhaps the fact that
the peasants' boat had no seats, and you had to stand balancing
yourself the whole trip, had something to do with it.

I was the first person off the boat, running down the wobbly
little gangplank with my stomach turning over with joy and
excitement at being back in this familiar, beloved spot. There
was Nils, the little hunchbacked driver, standing by his carriage, flicking his long whip in the dust, waiting for us. Nils
was quite young, and lived with his old mother and his
brothers right behind the church — actually in its dooryard.
The church was very old, and Nils' family had been there a
long time too, for their name was Kirkehus ("Church-house").

Nils, all misshapen four feet of him, was a dandy. No wooden peasant shoes for him, but black leather "city shoes," polished, under the dust. His legs, no longer than those of an eight-year-old, were encased in well-creased dark trousers, and the bright red or pink ties he always wore drew your eyes away from the distorted back under the neat navy blue jacket. He wore a black-visored cap set at a jaunty angle on the back of his head, a flower in his buttonhole, and held a large wooden match firmly between very white teeth, flipping it from side to side of the generous smiling mouth as he talked.

Nils drove a Stolkjerre, a carriage with two big wheels, used in the country, and he owned the only two for hire in the village. His little tan mountain ponies with the cream-colored tails and "crew-cut" manes were curried within an inch of their lives. Nils was the brains of his family: his brothers, who were young giants over six feet tall, were clods. I have also heard that Nils was a devil with the girls.

While the luggage was being loaded onto the carts, I ran up the hill just above the wharf to a low red house with a sod roof, and a small garden enclosed by a white picket fence. Behind the fence, silently watching me run up the path, stood a very old woman, hands folded under her striped blue apron. She had the kind of beautiful face that kindliness and a calm and cheerful acceptance of the vicissitudes of life had imprinted on her basically good features. Her white hair, showing beneath the triangular black shawl that older peasant women wore on their heads, was neatly parted and drawn back into a small bun. Elizabeth and I always had the same rather limited conversation, year after year.

"Yuss, Tutti," she would say, taking me in from head to heels. "And so here you are back from Amerika again, and how

tall you have grown." A slight pause, and then, "And have
you seen my Per in Amerika?"

Sorry to disappoint her, I answered sadly, "No, I haven't."
Elizabeth's son Per had left his mother's cottage thirty years
before, and settled in Minnesota, a place that was just a pink
square on the map to me.

"Well," she would say, "he has to stay and take care of that
big farm he owns, but maybe next year he will come." And
then dropping this subject, always so near to her heart, "Would
you like some Rips? They are just ripe now."

Back of Elizabeth's fence was a row of currant bushes, so
heavy with fruit that the branches curved downwards, their
tips touching the ground. She would select a particularly full
branch, and cutting it cleanly near the center stem, hold it out
to me, the berries hanging from it like a fringe of enormous
rubies, glinting in the sun.

"Oh, thank you so much, Elizabeth, I am glad to be back."
And carefully carrying my gift of jewels, I would return to the
waiting carriages.

Not only were the currants a feast to the eyes, but when we †
got home Karen would strip the ripe berries from their stems,
with a fork, put them in a bowl with plenty of sugar and a
vanilla bean, and let them "ripen" overnight. Tomorrow they
would be our dessert.

The luggage was finally loaded, with Karen and Sigrid
wedged in among boxes and bundles on the luggage cart.
Grandfather and I got into the first Stolkjerre, while Grandmother and Mother settled into the following one. Nils cracked
his whip and we started off on our trek up into the mountains.
The dogs ran behind, and since the road lay upward all the
way, they were often running ahead of the sturdy little ponies

who had such a load to pull. Out of the village, past the old
wooden church — no time today to stop and look at the primitive paintings of saints and angels, and decipher the Latin
inscriptions encircling the inside walls — on past the cherry
trees, branches laden with ripe fruit, bending over the stone
wall saying, "Help yourself" as we brushed by, and then we
were at the first of the many wooden gates across the road.
They were there to keep the cows in their proper pastures, and
Nils was only too happy to have me climb out and open them,
wait for all our carriages to pass through, then slip the heavy
wooden bar into place again.

There were two steep hills on the way up to the hut, and
Grandfather made us all get out and walk up them "to save
the horses." Even Nils came down from his perch and stalked
alongside on his spindly legs like a rather dapper sparrow,
leading the horses. Everyone walked except Mother, who refused to get out and trudge up the hill in her thin, beige, high-
heeled shoes. If it were even suggested to her, she would utter
one word, "Nonsense!" When Mother said "Nonsense!" in
that firm, slightly accented voice, that was the end of discussion.

We were finally nearing the halfway mark, a prosperous-
looking farm with wheat fields stretching out of sight, up to
and beyond the still distant river. The farm, which had lain
there for hundreds of years, and was the largest one in the
district, bore the name Valheim, and the family of that name
still lived there. It was of special interest to me, for this, in a
slight variation, was my grandfather's name.

One of the original owners had left his lands early in the
eighteenth century and gone to Bergen, where he established
himself as a merchant and eventually married the daughter
of a famous bishop, a power in the land at that time. We were
his direct descendants, and so we were actually returning to

the cradle of our family when we came back here to Årdal. The good-looking girls working in the fields, though somewhat heavy, bore a distinct resemblance to Mother, and the men had the characteristic thick, jutting eyebrows of Grandfather and all the uncles.

This was the last house, the last hill to climb before we reached Finnebu, and now we were up on the high plateau. Off on the left we could see the long narrow lake, sheer black mountains rising from its farther shore, and on the right was the river, still out of sight, but welcoming us with its distant roar.

At last the tired horses came to a full stop, we all got out of the carriages, and I flew down the little path through the birch grove and was first to come upon our beloved Finnebu. There it lay, hidden among the birch trees, unchanging from summer to summer, looking like the Hansel and Gretel house, minus the witch. The house was made of thick logs, peeled and oiled so long ago that they had mellowed to a dark browny black. The sod roof was a flowering field, thickly overgrown; the grass and flowers hung down over the low eaves making it look like a house in need of a haircut. On the sloping roof grew berries and bluebells and daisies and buttercups, and even some heather. By standing on tiptoe I could reach a patch of blueberry bushes over the small kitchen window. The curling pieces of birch bark, placed for insulation under all the sod, curved up like a festoon around the edge of the roof, and held the sod in place.

At the front of the house, facing the river, the two small dormers opening out of the upstairs bedrooms barely broke the expanse of the roof. They were like heavy-lidded eyes, lifting miniature roofs of their own over small-paned windows, and the grass and flowers growing up in front of them almost entirely obscured the view.

A raised wooden porch ran around two sides of the house, and on it were placed a few canvas easy chairs and a plain wooden well-weathered table. On the wall, above and beneath the windows, were rows of heavy metal hooks, placed horizontally about a foot apart. These were used to support the long flexible salmon rods when not in use, and there were also other hooks for the long-handled net, and the gaff with its wicked hook safeguarded by a cork.

The windows were bracketed by old shutters, painted pale green like the window trim, and hanging slightly askew. In the upper half of each was cut out a small heart. It was a house that you wanted to pick up and hug.

Inside, there was a good-sized low-ceilinged square room that served as living and dining room. Here the logs were also peeled and oiled, but, not being weathered like the ones outside, had kept a lighter hue. There was not very much furniture in the room, and what there was of it was well worn and comfortable. A long rough country table, used for eating, was between meals piled high with newspapers, English magazines, my water-color paints, Grandmother's embroidery, and Grandfather's pipes resting in a big ashtray. In back of the table, suspended by two strong hooks from a beam in the ceiling, was a long brown canvas porch swing, now firmly fastened to the wall behind it to keep it from swinging. It was piled high with bright-colored cushions, and served in lieu of a sofa. There were several high-backed rush-seated chairs that doubled as dining-room chairs, and two wicker armchairs, one on each side of a low round table with a kerosene lamp in the middle of it.

There was a small raised fireplace on one wall, with a stone chimney and mantel. Its low fender was usually festooned with drying socks and fishing gear.

Two built-in corner cupboards held the glasses, china, and silverware. These cupboards, and the doors, and a small hanging shelf holding tattered English novels and back numbers of the Fisherman's Manual, were painted in basic Norwegian peasant colors, which are not crude and garish, but soft and pleasant. The cupboards were a subdued bluish green, the bookshelf and the doors of the room a rosy-rusty red.

The low ceiling and old-fashioned small-paned windows made the room quite dark, but we were usually outdoors in the daytime, no matter what the weather. At night, with candles and kerosene lamps adding to the glow from the birch logs burning in the fireplace, it was snug and cozy and light.

There was a row of hooks on the far wall, and a great variety of fishing hats hanging from them: everyone's favorite headgear from time immemorial. There was an old battered Panama, and a topee (surely out of place in this damp climate!), a checkered English "racing-tout" cap, a moth-eaten blue beret, and several stained old brown felt hats. Most of the latter were Grandfather's although some of the cousins and friends who came here alone with him, "baching" it, left part of their gear behind. Grandfather's hats were gaily decorated with fishing flies that had either broken their points or, having caught a particularly fine salmon, were deemed worthy of being retired to the hatband.

On the top log of the wall above the big table, a dozen or more large fish tails were tacked up. This was the trophy wall. When anyone had caught a particularly large or "brave" fish, the tail was cut off short, dried in the sun, then tacked up on the wall with the fisherman's name, and any pertinent data like the weight, and what pool it was taken in, written on the log underneath. There was one enormous tail from the largest salmon ever caught in that river, with Grandfather's name underneath. And a middle-sized tail preserved because Uncle Thomas, on a rare visit home from South Africa, had hooked the fish late one evening, and played it all night, up and down a long stretch of river, finally tiring out the fish (and himself) after fourteen hours, and bringing it triumphantly in.

(Let me make a statement here and now about certain fishing terms: in Norway you "take" a salmon, in the British Isles it is strictly non-U to speak of anything but "killing" a salmon. I just *catch* a salmon, when I am lucky enough to do it. It seems simpler and less lethal that way.)

Off the living room was the bedroom that Mother and I shared. It had two rather narrow built-in bunks, a washbowl and pitcher on a stand in one corner, and gaily chintz-curtained low windows, opening outward directly onto the porch, and toward the river. It was fairly easy to escape Mother's vigilant eye and ear by bypassing the heavy squeaky bedroom door and stepping out lightly through the window whenever I decided the night was too lovely and light for sleeping. Sometimes I just sat on a rock in the river, listening to it roar as it swirled about me. Other times I would go across to the neighboring farmer's house and share their early breakfast. It is strange for anyone accustomed to a normally divided day of fairly equal hours of light and dark, to be suddenly in a place where there is no night at all. There is no feeling of daylight and nightfall governing either working hours or meals. It is all daylight, and all fluid. Sven, the peasant boy next door, having had his dinner around five in the afternoon, went on working at a leisurely pace in his father's fields for several hours more. Sometimes he would leave to go fishing with me; no need to milk the cows until nine or ten in the evening, then set the large milk pails in the river to cool until morning. Those at Finnebu who went out fishing seldom came home before eleven, sitting down on the porch to a leisurely drink in the suggestion of twilight, before having a bite of supper and turning in. By 2:00 A.M. it was daylight again.

There was a logbook kept since the early 1900s. It made fascinating reading: the flies had such lovely names. There were Silver Doctor and Black Doctor, Hunter White Wing and Claret Baron, and later on in the thirties, Wagtail and Cocktail and "Popham 9/0."

In the logbook were notations like this: "Ten-thirty P.M. Slightly cloudy. Caught twelve-pound salmon in Forked Pool on Jock Scott fly." Or, "Eleven-thirty P.M. Fine clear evening. No wind. Lost a huge fish in Sandpool after working an hour and a half with him. The fish remained steadily at the deep lower end of the pool, gradually working itself down until it was impossible to hold. Gut broke!" (Drama on the River under the Midnight Sun!)

The kitchen, just off the living room, at the back entrance to the house, was very small, dark, and primitive. There was a cupboard for staples, and a narrow wooden counter with a little round tin basin on it for dishwashing. The two pails, kept filled with fresh water from the river, stood on this counter too, each with a dipper hanging on the edge. The small black wood-burning stove had to be fed birch logs continually and was always either blazing hot or about to go out. In spite of these conditions, Karen managed to turn out superb meals.

"Oh, Karen, waffles for breakfast!" I exclaimed happily. †
"Could I have some of the wild strawberry jam with them?" †

And coming home ravenous for dinner, after a whole day out on the river, heading directly for the little kitchen, "Mm-mm, Kalvekarbonadekaker. I could eat a dozen right † now!" And I often did. These veal patties are the best meat cakes I know, and have the advantage of being equally good when reheated.

Sven's farm was just beyond the birch grove, so we always had the freshest of eggs and milk, and cream so thick it had
† to be served with a spoon. Tiny little plump chickens, too, came from there. They were even smaller than our present Cornish game hens, and so tender, simmered in the big black pot.

Since we always got there rather late on the day of our arrival, and there was much to do putting things away, water to be fetched from the river, food to be stored in the cool little cellar under the house, the first meal Karen made for us was
† something quick and simple: delicious bacon pancakes, or a
† bit of smoked fish we had brought with us from town, simmered in a little milk, and needing no other accompaniment than small new potatoes, boiled in their jackets — the first of his crop, left by our kind neighbor. There was also likely to be a basket of dark red morello cherries, from the same source. I sat on the porch railing after supper, trying to spit the pits as far as the river. They always fell short — halfway — like most of my aspirations.

"Now come to bed, dear," said Mother, coming out into the lovely late twilight. "It's been a long day, and it is past eleven o'clock."

"Please, Mother, *please,* can't I just run down to the river for one minute?"

"Well, go quickly then, and come right back. And be careful not to slip on the rocks."

The river. The all-encompassing river. The river was our way of life in Årdal. It slaked our thirst, it cooled our bodies and our beer and wine, and it provided our sport and entertainment. Finnebu not only would have had no excuse for being, it simply couldn't have existed without the river.

Like most Norwegian streams, it was a foaming, rushing torrent of crystal-clear icy water for the greater part of its length, and even in the calmer stretches, and the pools where the salmon lurked, the current flowed clear and strong beneath our feet. Its icy waters came from some high glacier, then emptied into the black lake a short distance from us, and pushing its way out through a narrow cut, it started its bounding journey on past Finnebu and down to the sea. Its noise, as it rushed over huge boulders, sending spume high in the air, was the music we lived by, but as it reached the beginning of the birch grove where the hut stood, it widened out and grew quieter. On the opposite bank it had at one time been diverted into a little mill, but while water still flowed glassily over the green mossy boards of the millrace, the diversion no longer served its purpose, for all that remained of the millhouse were four rotting posts. On our side, it grew quite shallow for a way, flowing in to our birch-grown shore over sand and among small boulders and rocks, weaving a pattern of many little streams and pools, where I could sometimes catch a small breakfast trout, not yet ready for the big river.   †

All bathing and washing, for such as I who disdained the pitcher and bowl set up in the bedroom, was done in the river. There was a sandy, quiet spot that seemed to hold the sun longer, and was a few degrees warmer than any other part, so was dubbed "The Bathtub." You announced loudly that you were going for a bath, and taking soap and large towel set bravely forth . . . but not to linger long! The warmth of the water in that spot was only relative. It was so cold that you not only tingled, but burned when you emerged.

Closer to shore was a tiny fall of water between two rocks, one of them large enough to crouch on with room to spare for washcloth and toothbrush without losing them in the river. It was the perfect place for teeth brushing, rather like the continual stream of water flowing into that white porcelain bowl at the dentist's, but prettier. When I came back years later with my husband and two sons, I was delighted to have the boys "discover" my teeth-brushing rock for themselves and put the little waterfall to the same use.

The outhouse was, of course, far from the river, on the other side of the hut, at the edge of the woods. It was an adjunct of the woodshed and was made of logs like the house, and had its own sod roof. Since the hook on the outhouse door was rather slack, it left a two-inch crack through which one could gaze out on the relaxing sight of cows browsing in the neighboring pasture.

There was a small cellar under the hytte, dug right into the peaty soil, and that was our "cool-room." But Grandmother would not allow the milk and butter to be kept there, she said they took on a queer "cellar taste," so along with the beer and the wine bottles cooling in the river within easy reach, were set the covered pail of milk and the butter, carefully wrapped in a piece of oiled silk.

Sometimes Karen would put some milk aside to sour slightly, and then pour it into glass bowls and place them on the windowsill for a day or two so that the milk could set. And so we † had Rømmekolle, a simple and refreshing dessert for a hot day. The top was a thick layer of cream, and the soured milk underneath had the consistency of junket. You were given your own individual bowl, sprinkled sugar and zwieback crumbs on top, and spooned up the smooth, creamy mixture with loving concentration. I suppose the nearest translation of Rømmekolle is clabber, but I prefer the British name of Bonnyclabber.

All water for cooking and washing up was fetched from the river in those two pails, and Sigrid went back and forth many times a day to replenish them. Water for washing the dishes (as well as the large pitcher of hot water we all received in our bedrooms in the evening) was heated on the same little wood-burning stove in the kitchen.

After finishing the day's work, Karen and Sigrid would sit out on the riverbank, Karen singing Salvation Army hymns, for she was an ardent and devoted member, while Sigrid accompanied her on the guitar. Grandfather would groan and say, if she wasn't such a good cook he wouldn't be able to stand it.

While Karen did all the cooking, it was Sigrid who made the beds, swept the hut, and spent hours on a rock at the river's edge, washing out our clothes and table linens with a strong-smelling green soap and a wooden paddle with which she pounded out the stains. She was also much in demand on the daily fishing trips, and my grandfather and his friends all said that when it came to gaffing and bringing ashore a still struggling salmon, there was no one to match Sigrid's skill. Grandmother was not very happy at having Sigrid taken away from her housework, and a typical conversation went like this:

"But, Wallem, she has to wash all your shirts and socks and the tablecloths — you simply cannot take her away fishing for the whole day."

"The shirts can wait. Do you want me to get a fine fish on, and then have no one to land it for me? By the time Petter or Halfdan or anyone else puts down his fishing rod and gets to me, the salmon is gone. Anyway, I promise to have her back in time to set the table for dinner. What are we having?"

"Veal Paprikash." This resignedly from Grandmother.   †

"Good! Plenty of potatoes, please. None of that rice or noodles nonsense!" And off he would go, Sigrid trailing behind him with gaff and net, delighted to have gotten out of her housework.

She was a very pretty pink-cheeked country girl in her early twenties, always neat and clean in a blue cotton dress, starched white apron, and her thick brown hair tied up in a white embroidered kerchief to keep it out of her eyes. For all her lack of sophistication, she had a certain aware look in the eye, a way of putting back her head and laughing whenever any man (except Grandfather, of whom she stood too much in awe) talked to her, as though she possessed some delicious secret all her own.

I remember one of "Mother's Officers," who had come for a few days of fishing with us. He looked at Sigrid who had just come out on the porch to tell Grandfather that we were almost out of beer, and with an instantly interested look murmured, *"Mmm-mm appetitlig!"* This is a wonderfully descriptive word, particularly when applied to a pretty girl, literally, "appetizing," but really, desirable, tantalizing, and voluptuously provocative, implying even more by the tone in which it is said. And it certainly applied to Sigrid.

I remember the moment clearly, for as soon as the officer said the word, the relaxed atmosphere underwent a subtle change, and all the grown-ups had quite different expressions on their faces. Grandmother became very busy counting the stitches in the sock she was knitting, Grandfather turned away, after a quick, stern look through his spectacles at the young man, Uncle Petter looked amused, and Mother looked slightly annoyed. And Sigrid? Sigrid just laughed the way she did when one of the peasant boys would pull her apron strings to tease her, and went back into the house.

Something out of the ordinary was buzzing around me. I ran off to the river to wash my hands for dinner.

Mother was an excellent fisherwoman, and would go off happily with her father or one of her brothers, carrying her light English fishing rod over her shoulder. She wore pale blue or green tweed skirts, with matching handknit sweaters, and a Marlene Dietrich type beige felt slouch hat. Grandfather would never let anyone go near a "pool" who was dressed in bright colors. The colors would catch the salmon's quick eye, and he would be off in a flash. White was also forbidden for this reason. It was supposed to be good luck to the departing fishermen for those left at home to spit after them, but we had modified this somewhat rude gesture by simply saying "too-ee, too-ee" as they left. If you spat, they never saw it anyway, so by being articulate you got credit for good will.

There is a story about Mother's wiles as a fisherwoman that became a legend at Finnebu.

One day the neighboring farmer reported a large salmon, seen in the river not far from us.

"It's standing in the pool just downriver from the bridge," he said. "It was there when I drove my cows across to pasture this morning."

Out went Grandfather, and the uncles, and each in turn fished that pool all day long, but not a rise did they get. From time to time they went up on the bridge to check and see if the fish was still there, and there he still was, the silvery sheen of his sides showing him sheltered near a big boulder in the middle of the river. Finally, in deep disgust, they gave up and came home for dinner in the late afternoon. Dinner over, Mother pushed back her chair.

"I think I'll have a go at that fish; I'll bet I can get him, and the light is just right now."

Out she went to the river to try her luck, quietly, quietly, not to frighten him. She cast and cast her line, way out into the middle of the stream, letting the fly drift down near the boulder. The pool lay quiet in the evening light . . . not a ripple, not a sign of a fish. She went up on the bridge to have a look . . . he must have gone . . . No, there he still was, a little farther under the big stone. Mother swore, having more than a bit of temper. And never one to be crossed, she picked up a stone lying at her feet, and threw it at him angrily. A flash of the tail, and he was gone.

Well, she thought, that's that. I'll just try a few casts a little farther along; maybe I can at least raise a trout. So back to the riverbank she went, and cast her line out. The fly drifted downstream, she began to reel in, and then suddenly something grabbed the hook, the line went zinging out with that solid buzz-saw sound that meant he was on and pulling hard. Back and forth he thrashed, once leaping high out of the water with a sideways twist of his head to try to get rid of that hook.

"Mr. Salmon," said Mother, "I sure woke you up, and this time you are not going to get away!" Her shouts brought the menfolk running, as she finally landed him. The next day, people came from all the neighboring farms to see the salmon that "that Ellinor" had caught by throwing a rock at him. Mother was very pleased with herself. Even the poor fish couldn't withstand her!

When someone did bring in a sizable salmon like that, which was by no means an everyday occurrence, it solved the problem of meals for the next few days. If it was a particularly large fine fish, Grandfather would send a piece away to be smoked, usually the center cut, as the flesh near the head is apt to be oily, and the tail piece too small to bother with.

If it was a medium-sized salmon, about eight or ten pounds, it was poached whole for dinner that same evening, or, if caught late at night, the next day. Until you have eaten a fine, firm freshly-caught salmon like this, poached, and served with a little melted butter poured over it, and plenty of chopped parsley or dill (that ubiquitous herb so appreciated in Scandinavia), you have missed one of the great gastronomical treats of the world: top quality, fresh-as-possible food, simply but perfectly prepared. (See page 178 for recipe for Poached Salmon.)

The salmon was accompanied by a platter of young vegetables picked that morning — baby carrots, tiny peas, a head of cauliflower in the center, and small boiled potatoes — and with this there was always a salad of cucumbers, sliced paper thin, and wilted for several hours in a dish with a weight on, to make them more digestible.

In the summer, in Norway, the salmon was our end-all and be-all, a way of life and living. It provided not only our finest sport, but was also our gastronomical mainstay.

There was always smoked salmon for breakfast, as an accompaniment to scrambled eggs. And sometimes, not instead of, but as an alternative to Røkelaks (smoked salmon) we had Gravlaks (marinated salmon). This is considered a great delicacy, although the smoked is more universally popular.

And sometimes, at a late supper in the long twilight, a beautiful piece of cold salmon was put on the table, accompanied either by Sour Cream Sauce, or a Sauce Verte. With it, of course, cucumber salad and slices of small, thin-skinned tomatoes sent in from the greenhouses of Stavanger. The growing season in Norway is too short to make growing tomatoes outdoors worthwhile, but the greenhouse tomatoes were delicious, fantastically expensive, and worth every penny.

Even the leftovers of fresh salmon have a quality all their own. I have mentioned the Fiske Kreteng that I liked so much,
† and there were even little fish cakes to be made out of leftover Kreteng!

And so, except for the skin and bones, every bit of the salmon was used, even his tail, if it was a good-sized one, to be tacked on the wall as a trophy.

Mother loved to go fishing with her family, but let one of her former admirers come in from the city to spend a few days, and she would suddenly become languid and feminine and totally disinterested in fishing. She got out of those sensible tweeds, and into a striped muslin skirt and a white sheer blouse with a ruffled jabot down the front, all of it pulled in tightly at her slender waist, with a wide leather belt. I remember her stretched out in a deck chair, a short distance from the hut, twisting the stem of a flower between her fingers, and looking down under half-closed lids at Major B. who sat on the mossy ground at her feet.

Major B. was the epitome of the European career officer, who always looked as though he were wearing a uniform, even when wearing a bathrobe. He had been in love with Mother from the time she was a young girl, long before she married my father and moved to America. Major B. was tall and slim, but stiff as a ramrod, both in bearing and manner. Mother said that the girls always suspected that he wore one of those "waist-pincher" corsets. His hair, a nondescript color, was short and bristling, his voice was monotonous, and his hands felt sort of mummified, like a piece of dried codfish. In other words, he was utterly lacking in charm, and his only assets were his devotion, and his ability to dance the waltz beautifully.

He was like a devoted dog, looking at Mother with faithful brown eyes. He always turned up at my grandparents' house in Stavanger the day we arrived from America, in full uniform, carrying a bouquet of red roses for Mother. Bowing stiffly from the waist as he presented them to her, he would say in that absurd, humorless voice, while never taking his eyes from her face, "You are more beautiful than ever, kjaere lille Frue, more beautiful each year!" Then he would notice me (he couldn't very well help it, since I had just come into the room, almost knocking over the coffee table in the process), and he would extend that dry-fish hand and say, "And how is our little lady from Philadelphia? A *big* girl this year!" (This was said in such a way I knew he didn't just mean *tall*.)

The particular day that I remember with glee was a day he was leaving us at Finnebu, having long outworn his welcome, at least as far as I was concerned. He was sitting on the ground at Mother's feet, dressed in his uniform, as he was about to return to the city. Mother was probably wishing, too, that Nils and the Stolkjerre would come and take him down to the boat, as she had had enough of sentimental strolls by the river, and all those soulful glances.

I was sitting on the porch railing drinking Pineapple Brus (a very rare form of soda pop), and discussing with Grandmother the possibility of having *both* pancakes and Catalani †
Kake for dessert, since we were just having Pytt i Panna †
for the main course at dinner. It was a hot afternoon, and the Major had placed Mother's long chair in the shade, right over at the edge of the woods, where he sat at her feet. As I watched, he began to move a bit restlessly, shifting his position on the ground as though suddenly finding it uncomfortable.

All of a sudden he rose abruptly to his feet, clutching at the seat of his rather tight uniform pants. His face became very red. The next thing we knew, to our utter astonishment, he was racing toward the river, throwing off uniform and underwear in his wild flight. We heard him swear a great Norwegian oath: "Devil dance me! ANTS!!!" as he discarded his undershorts and plunged into the river.

The ladies had the satisfaction — or perhaps the disappointment — of discovering that the Major did not wear the reputed corset.

Though I have no particular recollection of being lonely, ever, in Norway, I suppose there must have been times when I longed for someone my own age to play with. Perhaps the fact that I was an only child, and used to being by myself, made me accept this yearly isolation without too much question, although the tales that I heard from my classmates when I returned to Philadelphia in the autumn, of beach picnics on Cape Cod, and sailing with their friends off the coast of Maine, did make me aware that my summers were very different from those of my friends.

But then, in Årdal, I had Sven. Sven was exactly the same age as I, and this was about all we had in common to start with, for Sven was the son of the farmer down the road from Finnebu, the farmer who supplied us with milk and eggs and those succulent little chickens. Sven was a stolid, towheaded peasant boy, whose days were spent helping his father run the farm. I spent a great deal of time trying to lure him away from his duties, not always successfully, for Sven was stubborn, and also was born with a conscience.

It wasn't a very large family, just Sven, his older sister Jenny, his mother, and his father. Jenny was one of those unfortunate

women born to be a spinster. She had a long, narrow face,
placid, and with regular, quite good features. There was something primitive and archaic about her face and body, like a
figure from an early Italian painting — Giotto, or Cimabue —
and when she moved, or gave you her hand to thank you for
something, it was quite lifeless, as though she were propelled
through no spontaneity or volition of her own.

Old Svein, the father, was a funny gnarled little man, half
the size of his tall wife Kari. He had gone out to America —
Wisconsin, I think — to farm, when he was in his twenties, and
when he was already middle-aged, returned to Årdal to the
small farm where he was born, to marry and settle there for the
rest of his life. He was always delighted to have a chance to
air his English with me, but it was pretty well evaporated by
now, being reduced to one phrase that seemed to have left an
indelible impression on his mind: "Look at de pig! Look at
de pig! Her bane fat!" His family stood by admiringly while
Old Svein and I "conversed" in English.

And then there was Kari, Sven's mother, the kindest, most
giving person I have ever known. She was very tall and straight
with a spare, angular frame. She had round blue eyes, with
sparse, pale lashes. Her face was smooth, and her skin white
without a vestige of color in it — I suppose we would call it
pasty — and made even paler by the black kerchief that concealed her still dark red hair, and by the long dark gray or black
dresses she always wore. I was in and out of their farmhouse
constantly, but no matter what she was doing in the house, she
would stop and stand listening to me chatter in my "city" Norwegian, her hands folded across her stomach, her head slightly
to one side, and a bemused expression on her face as though I
were the most entertaining creature in the world. No matter
what I was telling her, whether about my school in America,

or the need for an extra liter of milk that day, she would shake
her head in slow wonder as I talked, all the while murmuring,
"Ah, thou Tutti, thou Tutti!" as though I were somebody quite
extraordinary. I don't remember her venturing any opinions,
but she always listened, really listened to me, most gratifying to
a child.

Kari could never bear to have me leave her house without
giving me something out of her small store of things, usually
something edible: berries just picked from the bushes by the
kitchen stoop, a newly fried potato pancake with butter on it,
or waffles, four or five small heart-shaped ones, stacked on a
plate, generously sprinkled with sugar between the waffles.
Sometimes, when there was nothing there that she thought
would tempt me, she would go to her basket of just-gathered
eggs, lovely big pale brown ones, carefully select one, and hold
it out to me hesitatingly, cupped in both of her big hands, as
though she were offering me a precious piece of china. I was
always delighted with my own special egg.

"Oh, thank you, Kari, I'll ask Karen to boil it for supper for
my very own."

Even when Kari offered me that staple of peasant fare, Lefse,
a kind of limp, tepid, floury pancake that tasted exactly like
boiled flannel, I managed to choke it down. She was so kind
to me I couldn't bear to hurt her. And I can't bear to give you
the recipe for Lefse, but have given you the one for potato pancakes.

The peasants seemed very matter of fact and completely un-
emotional, although on rare occasions, so rare that they stand
out in my mind, there would be a slight display of what lay
underneath, some sort of expression of their relationship with
us city people from "away," and sometimes, very rarely, there

was a glimpse of quick, dry humor. But on the whole, dignity, not gaiety, was their outstanding characteristic.

In all the years that I ran in and out of Kari and Old Svein's farm, and involved myself in their daily lives, whether it was haying, or grafting apple trees, or just running to look at the new calf in the barn, they never allowed themselves to become emotionally involved with me. When we arrived each summer, there would be a hand hastily wiped on skirt or trousers, stiffly extended in greeting with a "So you're back from America," as though we had just stepped around the corner for a few days. Then they would go on with their chores, while I, terribly excited at being back, would run from house to orchard to barn, all the while carrying on a running conversation with them at the top of my lungs, while they silently watched me, like passive cows in a field staring at some sudden interloper.

When we left, it was the same thing; the hands again briefly extended and quickly withdrawn with a "Ja, ja, so you are off to Amerika again." I think the "ja, ja" designated a certain resignation, an acknowledgment of the fact that we were free to come and go as we pleased, but they were bound irrevocably to the farm and their animals, and their lives would continue unchanging from day to day.

The peasants' dialect, Landsmål (the country language) varies in different parts of the country, and many of the words bear no relation to the Riksmål (the national language) that we from the city spoke. As a child I soon grew used to the Årdal dialect, and picked up quite a few of their expressions in the course of a summer, much to the amusement of all my family except Bestemor, who thought it "coarse."

Yet their formality with us did not extend to the language, for they addressed all of us — even Bestefar, the patriarch — by our first names, and with the familiar *du*.

Considering the steady diet of bread, potatoes, and coffee that they lived on, the peasants were certainly durable. You often saw old men well into their eighties still working in the fields. Once, as we passed a farm on our way upriver to fish, Mother called out a greeting to Old Lars, out raking his hayfield, and known to be ninety-two years old. And she waved to him prettily. The following day we passed by there again.

"Well, Gamle Lars," Mother called out to him, "how are you today?"

Old Lars walked across to where we stood, and leaning on his rake looked straight at Mother, then said, with rueful admiration in his faded blue eyes,

"To tell you the truth, Ellinor, I tossed and turned and didn't sleep a wink all night, just for thinking of you."

Sven looked like his tall fair-skinned mother. He had inherited her solid frame, and from her the round blue eyes set in his pale freckled face. But while his mother's almost lashless eyes gave her an open, unguarded look, Sven's had very thick, very blond lashes, a screen between you and any expression his eyes might have held. Apart from this, his hair was dusty blond, and he looked like any small peasant boy on any farm for miles around.

He always wore, even on the hottest midsummer days, thick black wool trousers reaching about halfway down the calf, a dark cotton shirt, and a much battered and faded old black cap with a cracked patent leather visor, that someone must have bequeathed him from the assortment at Finnebu. And of course he always wore the clumsy wooden shoes, replaced on Sundays by leather-topped ones with heavy wooden soles. On Sunday he wore a complete heavy black suit, a light shirt, and the bright-colored tie I brought him every year from America. It was the one spot of color in all that Sunday-black-clad family.

Sven was by no means the ideal companion, had I had any choice (which I didn't). He was not very imaginative and certainly not loquacious. He had the same temperament as the plodding, stubborn little mountain ponies on his father's farm. But he was a faithful friend, he was my age — and he was there. For me, he became simply an extension of my summer self.

I don't remember when I first met Sven. I suppose I began to be allowed to take the milk pail and go and fetch the milk from Old Svein when I was about eight or nine, and Sven was there, utterly silent, and we probably just stood and stared at each other while the pail was being filled. It must have been the summer we were ten that Sven made me my first pair of wooden shoes. He looked disparagingly at my white sneakers one day, squishing around in the barnyard mud after a rainstorm, and said,

"If you are going to run around the farm all the time, you need some wooden shoes." I thought that was a good idea, then I wouldn't have to listen to Sigrid groaning anymore as she tried to get the day's muck off my sneakers.

"But where will I get them?" I asked.

"Oh, I expect I can make you some, the way I do my own. Here, put your foot on this log I just split, I'll draw around it." And taking an old stub of pencil out of his pocket, he drew a rough outline. When I came over the next morning, there he was, working away at my shoes in the little lean-to woodshed. They were still only roughly shaped with the ax, and looked enormous, so I was disappointed. But then he set to work on them with his knife, the good, straight, heavy-bladed, wooden-handled Tollekniv that every Norwegian boy carried, and by evening they were finished, smoothly and nicely, both inside and out. They were open at the back, and there was a slight heel. The toes were rounded, and did not turn up as much as Dutch wooden shoes, otherwise I think they were much the same.

I was delighted with them, but it took me some time to learn to keep them on my feet. It was rather like wearing very heavy scuffs, and you had to sort of curl your toes under, to keep them on. I never did manage to run in them, or leap from rock to rock in the river the way Sven did, but they were very useful when the grass and heather were still dewy in the early morning, or for getting through a muddy spot.

It became a custom for Sven always to make me a new pair, the first days after my arrival in Årdal every summer. Unfortunately, they were always left behind, but now you can buy something like them in many shoe stores in this country. They have been refined with leather tops, like the peasants' Sunday shoes, and come in bright colors. I keep a pair to wear in my garden, if I am out in the morning while the grass is still wet with dew. I find I can still walk quite comfortably in them by curling my toes under, just the way I used to in Årdal many years ago.

Certainly our diversions were of the simplest, but we had all outdoors, fields, river, and mountains to explore. If it was a good day for fishing, not too clear and sunny, but slightly overcast, I would pick up my bamboo rod and go in search of Sven. The fishing grown-ups had already gone off for the day to their favorite pools, the ones they leased every summer from the peasants who owned the land that the river ran through. It seemed ironical that a peasant was never allowed to fish for salmon in any part of the river, even though it was bordered by his fields. As long as the river was leased, only the lessee and invited friends could fish it. We had leased the greater part of the river for so many years that I took it for granted, as a child, that the whole river belonged to us. There were three excellent pools, Sandpool, Forked Pool (where a pretty little birch-grown island divided the rushing river), and Bergeland Pool. The latter lay directly across the river from Finnebu, so we could watch from the hut and if Grandfather or someone else hooked a fish, all he had to do was yell loudly to be heard above the river's roar, and someone with gaff and net would go rushing out of the house, up the road and over the bridge, to help land it. This pool, however, was the first to be deserted if the river was low, as it was quite shallow — not like "Sandpool" which was so swift and deep you couldn't see the bottom at all.

But Sven and I were relegated to the small streams or out-of-the-way parts of the river where we would disturb no one, neither man nor fish. Once I suggested to Sven that we go and fish from the nice grassy bank bordering the river just at the end of his father's potato field.

"You can go if you like," he replied, reddening slightly and looking down at his feet. "You know I can't. Sandpool lies just above our field."

Momentary embarrassment on my part and a confused feeling made me blush too. I had overstepped the line between us, and I had caused the first awkward moment between us. There was never any feeling of inequality: we simply accepted one another as companions who, for a certain time each year, during the lovely green days of our childhood, enjoyed doing certain things together because we were both the same age. When I look back on it I don't recall a single incident involving the difference in our social positions or sexes. Whatever romantic feelings, if any, I may have aroused in Sven's stolid being, he gave me no sign of it, and I never gave it a thought.

As far as I can recall there was little poaching of salmon on the part of the peasants, at least, when we were in residence. It must have been frustrating for them to see a fine fish waggling its tail at them just off their land and not be able to have a go at it, particularly since it would fetch a good high price at the market in town.

So Sven and I would go off fishing in quite a different direction. We had no reels on our simple bamboo poles; we simply wound the excess green line around one hand, in order to have something to let out if we were lucky enough to hook a trout. What would have happened with this arrangement if we had ever gotten a sizable fish on, I shudder to think.

We had our own favorite small pools and streams, some near home, but most farther afield. I was continually trying to overcome Sven's conscience and sneak him away from his chores for a few hours.

"Let's go up to Whale Pool," I would propose. "We could get there in twenty minutes on your bike, and I'll give you one of the new trout flies Bestefar got me. They just came in this morning with the groceries on the boat from Stavanger."

Poor Sven would look dubious, for he knew very well that with me sitting like a lump on the bar of his bike, it would take him a good forty minutes to peddle us to Whale Pool, and it was uphill all the way. But he would like to try one of the new flies; he'd lost several of his own lately . . .

"All right," he would finally answer, "but you'll have to hold both our poles, and try not to poke me in the eye with them this time."

"Whale Pool," my own name for it, was worth the uphill trip to get to it. It lay at a point where river and road ran parallel for a brief spell, only a short distance apart. Around a curve, and suddenly you came upon an enormous, smooth, dark gray rock, a great glacial boulder about sixty feet long, and high enough to quite conceal the water on the other side of it. Left there by the Ice Age, millenniums ago, it looked as though a giant whale had been caught at the edge of the river and had petrified through the ages, gradually sinking deeper into its bed of surrounding moss and heather.

I suppose it rose about twelve or fifteen feet at its highest point in the middle. There were little crevices on its smooth side that made easy footholds for climbing, and on its quite flat top, surrounded by soft gray-green moss and lichen, was an absolutely absurdly beautiful little lake. It was about fifteen feet long, and only three or four feet wide — a pretty, twisting shape, following the line of the fissure in the rock that gave it birth. It was like something out of a miniature Japanese garden, with little red highland cranberries, and just a few low blueberry bushes growing in the moss, and even a small stunted birch tree that had managed to find a foothold and was mirrored in its unruffled surface. Some tiny minnows had found their way into it, and swam frantically about when we stirred them up with a bare toe. The water, only a foot or two deep, was deliciously warm after the icy river I was used to. We sat there for a few minutes, dabbling our feet, eating a few of the blueberries near at hand, and looking down into the lazy flow of the river below us, to see if we could spot a trout hidden in the pool among the camouflaging gray rocks.

"Well, if we're going to fish, let's fish," said Sven, who was not much of a one for admiring the scenery. It was a beautiful pool, just too small for the salmon-fishing grown-ups, but large enough to sometimes harbor a good-sized trout, twice the size of the little fingerlings we caught so easily in the small streams nearer home. Sven and I would stand there for hours, fishing, each at our end of the Whale, not talking (Grandfather had trained me so strictly that to this day I still whisper if I'm within a hundred yards of any angler!), and when we'd had enough of it, by silent consent we climbed down from our Whale, often fishless, and headed for home. If we had been lucky enough to catch a couple of trout, Sven would cut a good strong Y-shaped birch branch, trim it down to a strong center stem and the two arms, which we would pass in through the fish's gills and out his mouth. Holding it proudly, I would climb onto my precarious perch on the bicycle bar, and Sven would whiz us home in no time at all, downhill all the way.

Once at Whale Pool, the summer I was twelve and had graduated to a small reel on my bamboo pole, I had only cast my line out half a dozen times, when I got such a yank on it I nearly went off into the river. My reel started spinning madly, the line going out with a minor imitation of that strident hum Grandfather's big reel made.

"Sven! I must have a salmon on! Come quickly! What shall I do?"

All this in a helpless feminine voice, for I suddenly realized I hadn't a clue as to proper salmon-fishing procedure. For years I'd tagged along after the grown-ups, watching them fish for a while, and getting bored and wandering away to diversions of my own. Nobody had ever thought it worthwhile to teach me what to do. When I went fishing, I just copied the motions the others went through, and Grandfather had shown me how to cast, once or twice, on the grass in front of Finnebu. But I had no idea how to play a fish like the one I had just hooked.

Sven came clumping over to me on wooden shoes.

"Don't let your line out so far . . . he'll go behind that big rock and break the leader off. Then you'll lose the fish *and* your fly!"

(To Sven a fish was just a fish, but a fly cost money.)

"How will I ever land him?" I asked, pushing the catch down as the tip of the rod bent madly, and the fish plunged out again into midstream. We never bothered to bring a net for the small trout we usually caught.

"Just you get him in to shore. I'll land him for you."

With which Sven went off into a clump of birch trees, leaving me to struggle on alone with my fish without even the comfort of his presence. I was torn by several fears: first, that I would lose my fish, and secondly, that I would lose my none-too-secure foothold on the big smooth rock, and plunge into the icy river, rod and all. Of course there was no question of not going in with the rod; the captain goes down with his ship.

By this time I was getting tired, my arms were aching, and I thought Sven would never come back from whatever he was doing with the birch branches he had cut. Fortunately for me, the fish must have been tired of fighting this very amateur fisherman too, so there was more line being reeled in, without those terrible sudden pulls out again. And Sven did appear just as I could see the fish below me (not half as large a monster as I had imagined), carrying a sort of half-hammock he had somehow managed to fashion out of the leafy green branches. Carefully he half climbed, half slid down the rock on his wooden shoes, and after one more sudden spurt of rebellion on the part of my fish, I managed to bring him in close enough for Sven to scoop him up in the birch basket and literally hurl him up onto the top of the rock, where he landed at my feet. I promptly sat on him to keep him from plopping back into the river, as he was still very lively and many a fish has escaped by playing possum for a minute, then suddenly jumping back to freedom in the water. I was not taking any chances. My first salmon!

Sven found a rock and gave him a good thump on the head to kill him, after which we bundled him into his birch-bough litter again and set off for home with me perched unsteadily on the bicycle bar, cradling my prize, while Sven, with this added impediment, wobbled all over the road.

We just about made it to Finnebu, where I almost fell off the bicycle in my excitement, and with the briefest of farewells to Sven, rushed up onto the porch and dropped my catch onto the table in the midst of my elders who were sitting around relaxing with a Scotch-and-seltzer after an unrewarding day on the river.

"Please, Grandfather," I begged, "please weigh him right away. He *is* a salmon, isn't he, and not just a grilse?"

In Norway there is a saying, "A favorite child has many names," and the beautiful salmon certainly qualifies. He starts out in life a fry, or fingerling, graduates to parr or smolt, leaves the river and goes out to sea. Now an adult he comes back to the river for the first time, to spawn, and he's called a grilse, the last step before he's a full-sized salmon, weighing over six pounds.

When a fish of indeterminate size was brought home, he was immediately put on the scales, and according to the result the fisherman would either proclaim (trying not to show his satisfaction too much) "a fine salmon, seven and a half pounds!" or (slightly defensively), "a beautiful grilse, just under six pounds, and a very gamy one too . . . gave me quite a fight there for a few minutes!" It was like having to settle for a girl, when you'd had your hopes set on a bouncing baby boy.

Grandfather was busy hanging his green fishing line over the railing to dry. When he finally turned around and took a look over his spectacles at what I had laid on the table, he looked quite surprised.

"Whale Pool," he said. "Haven't been up there for a long time. Caught him on a trout fly, did you?"

"Yes, Grandfather," I answered, nodding vigorously and hopping about. Wouldn't he ever put him on the scales? "One of the new ones you got me."

"It must have been that bit of red that caught his eye." He bent over examining the fish. "And you had him well hooked too. I can see by his mouth you had quite a time getting your fly back from him."

"Oh, I'm sure she got Sven to take the hook out of his mouth," said my mother, who never believed in doing for herself what she could get some man to do for her.

"Oh, no!" I cried.

(Of *course* Sven had removed the hook for me, and almost had to break the fish's jaw to do it, but I wasn't about to admit to everybody that I didn't do it myself. Getting the little barbed hook out of a gaping fish-mouth, as well as cleaning out all those nasty insides, were tasks that Sven took upon himself to do for me, unquestioningly. I wasn't my mother's daughter for nothing.)

Grandfather settled his spectacles more firmly on the end of his nose, then picking up my fish by the gills with one hand, walked over and took down the brass scales with the big hook on the end, from the back of the porch door where they were kept handy to weigh the day's catch. Standing with his back to me, he hung my fish on the hook, while I held my breath, closed my eyes, and prayed as I only did in moments of great stress.

"Please, God, please, let him be over six pounds and his tail can go up on the wall with the others, and I'll never answer Mother back again . . . or anything, just please let him be a salmon, not just a grilse."

"A fine young salmon . . . just under seven pounds," and Grandfather hung the scale back on its nail and carried my fish back to the porch table. With a quick "Thank you, God, amen," I let out my breath.

"Congratulations," said Grandfather. "Maybe you'll be as good a fisherwoman as your mother someday." He took out his big pocket knife and cut off the tail cleanly with one hard stroke.

"This one must go on the wall," he said. "But tell me, Tutti," as we started indoors to look for thumbtacks, "where did you stand, and how did you manage to land him in that place? As I remember, although I haven't fished your Whale Pool for many years, the rock is very slippery . . . there isn't really any flat place to land a fish, and the river there is very deep and swift." He bent a worried look on me for a moment, then went on with the business of tacking up the fish tail.

"Oh, we managed all right," I said, and disappeared quickly into the kitchen, where I handed over my tailless fish to Karen. I knew what he meant, and was suddenly guilt-stricken; Sven couldn't swim a stroke, and my prowess in that field was nothing to count on. Sven, in his heavy black suit, would have sunk like a stone, and I wouldn't have had much chance in that icy current myself.

The nice thing about grandparents was that they didn't insist on how dangerous things you did were, the way a parent did. Mother would carry on as though I were already drowned, just at the sight of me leaping from stone to stone out in the river. Whereas grandparents were much more advanced; they'd been through all that with their own children, and had learned that tentative danger is a natural perquisite of youth, and continuous warnings fall on totally deaf ears.

We stuck my fish tail right up next to Uncle Petter's last one,

and Grandfather wrote underneath on the smooth log, in his
fine slanted handwriting, TUTTI. FIRST SALMON. WHALE POOL.
With the date and weight following. It was a terribly proud
moment.

We had my fish for dinner that evening. Everyone exclaimed
that it was the best salmon they had ever eaten, but I thought it
fortunate that Karen had made a good thick Yellow Pea Soup †
as a first course, as the fish, when it was brought in on the
platter, appeared smaller than I had remembered it. Did it
really weigh seven pounds? Grandfather had said it did, even
though I didn't actually see the scales when he weighed it.

Much of the time Sven was too busy helping his father on
the farm to play with me, and I would tag after him as he fed
the livestock, or mended fences, or pulled potatoes. I particularly liked taking part in this latter job, as all the useless little
potatoes — the ones no bigger than a walnut that the peasants †
discarded, or gave to the pigs — were put aside for me to take
home. Karen would scrub them and boil them for supper.
They would come to the table in a big blue and white china
bowl, their pale, thin brown skins shining matly underneath
the sour cream she had poured over them. With a thin slice of
ham or a piece of cold salmon, this made a good supper dish.

And we always had them with a Bif à la Lindstrøm, a recipe †
given Mother by a famous and admiring Swedish actor.

I didn't know it then, but this was the last summer that we
would spend any length of time at Finnebu. Mother had been
away a lot that summer, leaving me with Grandfather and
Grandmother, Karen and Sigrid. When she came back from
these trips, she complained more and more that even for a
fishing hut up in the mountains, Finnebu was too small and

primitive, that her bedroom was most uncomfortable — the fact that she shared it with me, I must admit, had its drawbacks, as I had a habit of bringing in frogs, kittens, even a nest of field mice abandoned by their mother, to share the room with us. And, she went on, the kitchen was a black hole. It *was* pretty dark, and not large, or at all modern, but considering all the delicious meals Karen managed to turn out of it, I felt called upon to defend it. It was familiar, and I loved it.

"But it's such a nice cozy kitchen, Mother, and the birch wood burning in the stove makes such a nice crackly sound and
† smells so good. Karen is making blueberry fritters tonight."

"An electric stove would be much easier for Karen," said Mother, "and if we had a summer house with electricity in it, you wouldn't ruin your eyes reading by that old kerosene lamp. You know how fussy your father is about your eyes." (Why did she suddenly bring my father into it, I wondered.)

"I think it would be nice to live over by the lake," she continued. "Sometimes I wish I could turn this noisy river off!" Turn our lovely river off! Whatever had gotten into Mother? Children instinctively dread any change in their daily life, so I resolutely dismissed this conversation from my mind, and went to watch Karen dropping the plump little fritters into deep fat in the big black kettle.

Then one weekend, a man with a large blond mustache, and a very loud commanding voice, came to spend a few days with us at Finnebu. The mustache only partly concealed the wide curving mouth, which together with a long nose and strong white teeth made him look exactly like the wolf in my old book of fairy tales. He was quite jovial, and his manner was affable, but there was a note of authority in his voice that gave the immediate impression of a big man used to giving orders and being instantly obeyed. Dressed in heavy English tweeds, with a cap to match, and carrying a walking stick with a gold band around it, he got down from Nils Kirkehus' Stolkjerre, flung directions over his shoulder to bring the heavy leather portmanteau and his fishing rods to the house, and went immediately to my mother, who was sitting on the porch railing affecting an air of complete dispassion about this arrival. Bending over her he picked up her purposefully limp hand, brushed the back of it quickly with his blond mustache, and lingered a moment to murmur something that made her laugh and blush slightly. Then he went directly to my grandparents, embracing both of them fondly. I stood and gaped at him. Enter the villain!

"Well, Harald, velkommen to Finnebu," said Grandfather. "It's certainly a long time since we have seen you. How long? Twenty years?"

"Twenty-two, to be exact," said our visitor, "since my father sent me out to Shanghai to take care of his business there."

He suddenly discovered me standing there staring at him, and stared back with raised eyebrows as though to demand who I was, and what I was doing there.

"Tutti," said Grandmother hastily, "come say how-do-you-do to your Uncle Harald." He was a relative!

"This is Ellinor's daughter," said Grandmother, as I bobbed a curtsy.

My new-found relative reached into his vest pocket and brought out from it a single round piece of glass with a long black ribbon hanging from the rim. With some difficulty he managed to establish it in his left eye. He peered at me through the glass as though I were a bug on a pin, and I stared right back, fascinated to discover that the glass made his left eye seem much larger than his naked right eye, and gave him a wickedly misproportioned look.

"So this is Tutti," he said, removing the glass from his eye. "Well, she's a nice *big* girl, isn't she? I suppose she takes after that American, her father." He turned his wolfish grin on Mother. "She certainly doesn't look like her mother, does she?"

Mother made matters worse in my eyes, by saying as though she were defending me, "Well, when she wears blue, people say her eyes are like mine."

"They are not! They're green!" I burst out, and fled to my bedroom, furiously determined to throw out every piece of blue clothing I possessed.

But then, being there, and the window being open, I allowed my curiosity to overcome my outrage, and listened to the conversation as it continued.

This Uncle Harald was a relative, but how close a relative I couldn't make out. Really a cousin of sorts, I decided. He had become rich and successful in the Orient, and now maintained an office and a house in Oslo too, and tried to get back as often as he could to "keep in touch with Norway."

He was on one of his keeping-in-touch trips this summer, and had met Mother at a ball earlier in the month in Oslo. He hadn't seen her since she was a child.

"And Father," she said, "when I told him you were in here fishing, he begged to be allowed to come for a few days and see you and Mother again, and the land the family came from. And to try for a salmon. I hope our river won't disappoint him."

"No, no, you are most welcome, Harald," said Grandfather, "and you will get your salmon. You will see."

In the days that followed, Uncle Harald did go fishing once with Grandfather, but mostly he and Mother spent a great deal of time going for long purposeful walks by the lake. They would come back with enthusiastic accounts of the superiority

of the higher land that rose from the lake to the low land by
the river that Finnebu was built on.

Finally one day Grandmother and Grandfather were per-
suaded to go walking with Mother and Uncle Harald. Nobody
asked me to come along; I went off to see what Sven was doing.

When I came home, just before dinner, they were all sitting
on the porch around an open bottle of champagne, one of several that Uncle Harald had brought, and that had been lying
cooling in the river until now. There were many skåls and
toasts to each other, and Mother and Uncle Harald were looking terribly pleased with themselves and with the world in
general.

"Can I have some champagne?" I asked Mother.

"Of course! Of course!" said Uncle Harald boisterously.
"Tutti must have a glass too." And he poured a large glassful
for me.

"Skål, Tutti," said Mother, "skål to the new property and its
new owner!" And she raised her glass and looked at Uncle
Harald with wide-open blue eyes.

It was explained to me that Uncle Harald had fallen in love
with this part of the country, and was especially determined to
buy part of the property of his ancestors. He and Mother had
spent days looking for just the ideal site for a house, and today
he had finally bought a piece of land over by the lake, and the
building of a house there would start immediately, before bad
weather set in.

"The new house will be ultramodern inside," said Uncle
Harald, "but outside it will look like an old Norwegian hytte
that might always have been there. And there will be plenty of
room for guests. What do you say to that, Uncle Michael?"
addressing Grandfather.

"Sounds fine," said Grandfather, who was perfectly happy at

Finnebu, but believed in letting others have their say and their way as long as it didn't discommode him.

It wasn't until several weeks later, when Mother and I were on our way back to America, that she explained to me one day, as we sat in our deck chairs on the boat, how kind Uncle Harald was, for Uncle Harald was so fond of Grandmother and Grandfather, that he wanted them to be more comfortable when they came in to Årdal to fish. So, although the house he was building was for his own use whenever he could get away from his business affairs, he had invited Grandmother and Grandfather to spend their summers there from then on, as long as they lived. Now wasn't that a nice thing to do?

And of course, when Mother and I came back to visit them, we would stay there too.

I was dismayed, but I knew there was no use in saying anything if this was what the grown-ups had decided. Well, I thought, I'll be able to walk over to Finnebu. And I'll see Sven. Maybe it will all be the same.

But it didn't work out that way, and over the years Finnebu and Sven became less and less a part of my life. I did not come back to reclaim them until many years later, when I was married and had children of my own. We arrived in Årdal on a beautiful day in midsummer, my husband and our two sons, aged ten and twelve. Finnebu lay there, lovely as always; unchanged. The farm too was much the same. Only Old Svein was gone.

Sven had the entire responsibility of the farm now. He had married a girl from farther up the river, and had three small childen. He had built a new shed, the potato patch was larger, there was an additional cow in the barn, and more fruit trees had been planted in the orchard.

Kari, his mother, was very old now, and seemed small for the

first time. When she sat on a bench outdoors, the sun still
caught glints of red in her thin, gray hair. She had put on the
black and silver shawl I had just brought her from America,
and sat there with idle, folded hands, like a very old doll, put
on exhibition.

Sister was still a long-faced spinster. Sven looked much the
same, although the old black cap had been discarded.

"Well, Tutti," he said, with a faint twinkle in his eye that I
had never noticed before, "I see you went and got yourself a
fine American husband, eh?"

"Yes," I said, and I grinned.

We had been told, on our way up to Finnebu, that the old
law forbidding the peasants to fish the river from their own
land had just been rescinded the past week. This was news
indeed, but since we no longer held the river rights since the
death of my grandparents, except for the stretch directly in
front of Finnebu, it didn't affect us very much.

A couple of evenings after we got there, I saw Sven in the
distance, new salmon rod over his shoulder, going off across his
fields to the stretch of river below the potato patch. High time,
thought I, after all these years, and I silently wished him luck,
and said "too-ee" in his direction.

The next day Sigrid, who was now with us in the capacity
of cook, came in with the early morning tea, and announced,
"Sven got a big salmon last night . . . eighteen pounds. Pretty
good for his first one!"

I was terribly pleased for him. I knew that Sven and his
family could never afford the luxury of eating the fish themselves, since prices for salmon in the market were astronomical
that summer, and he would be obliged to send it to Stavanger
immediately, to be sold. I asked Sigrid to go over right after
breakfast, and discreetly inquire if Sven would sell us at least

a part of it. I was sitting on the porch when she came back. "Well, what did he say?" I asked.

Sigrid looked very mysterious and said to me, "Now don't you ask about that fish anymore. Just stay where you are. I think you're about to have a caller." And she disappeared into the house.

Ten minutes later Sven appeared, formally dressed in his black suit, and carrying a new hat, prototype of the old black one. He stood below me, one foot on the bottom porch step, twiddling his hat in his fingers.

"Nice day," he began. "I just wanted to tell you that there's a new wire fence has been put up at the top of the hill where the big rock is. You have to go along the road a bit further, before you can cut down to Sandpool."

"Oh, thank you, Sven. As a matter of fact I was thinking of taking the boys over that way this afternoon so they could see where their great-grandfather used to fish."

Silence: I wasn't half as patient about these preliminaries as Sven was.

"By the way," I said, trying to sound casual, since that was the way he wanted it, and at the same time to give him an opening. "By the way, didn't I hear that you caught a big one down off the lower field last night?"

A very slight smile spread over Sven's broad face.

"Oh, yes, I did. Weighed over eight kilos." He took a deep breath. "Since it's my first one," he said, looking at me out of those fringed blue eyes, "I'm not going to send it to town. *You're* to have half of it as a present. Bring Sigrid to cut it . . . she knows how. I'll go get the knife." And before I could utter my mingled protest and heartfelt thanks, he had turned and gone back to his farm.

I was quite overwhelmed. How could I accept such an ex-

travagant gift? I went to Sigrid, who had an understanding
soul and said that of course I must accept it as a gift. Sven was
so pleased that this had happened while I was there.

So I got out of my blue jeans, put on a dress to do honor to
the occasion, and assembled my somewhat mystified family.
Then, with husband and sons in tow, and Sigrid following after
with a sacrificial-looking platter, we all went through the birch
grove over to the farm. As we arrived at the house, Sven's
oldest daughter dashed into the big cellar, and loudly announced our arrival to her family: "Amerikanerne kommer!"
(Sort of a "Lafayette, we are here" entrance.) We went in
through the wide, low cellar opening, and came upon a scene
that looked like a cross between a Japanese tea ceremony, and
some ancient Druid rites. On a long wooden table, set out
in the exact center of the cellar, lay the magnificent silver
fish. Someone — perhaps the children — had cut fresh birch
branches, and tucked them under and around him, the green
leaves giving him a very elegant look, as though he were being
served up on a bed of super-parsley. Lined up on the far side
of the long table stood Sven, a large knife in his hand, and all
his family beside him. Sven's wife and Kari and Sister all had
their American shawls on, so new looking that I felt I must
have forgotten to remove pins and price tags. Sven's two older
children were clutching the edge of the table, peering at the
fish which lay staring back at them, right on a level with their
eyes. Even the baby on its mother's arm opened wide eyes at
the unaccustomed goings-on.

I lined up on the other side of the table with Sigrid and my
family, and we all spoke at once, admiringly, of the fish: how
fat . . . how silvery . . . even a few sea lice still clinging to
him, showing he was fresh up from the sea, not long in the
river. A most beautiful fish! Even though my husband and

sons spoke a different language, there was no mistaking the admiration in their voices.

After several minutes of enjoying this adulation, Sven went around the table and with a slight bow handed the knife to Sigrid.

"Now you go ahead and cut a good half for Tutti — whichever half she wants."

Sigrid, who was nobody's fool, didn't even wait to consult me. Leaning over the table she measured off with the knife a large piece, right smack in the center of the salmon, the very choicest part!

"Tutti would like this piece," she said, as without more ado she neatly chopped off the head and tail pieces, pushed them aside, and laid the large center cut on the platter.

I was appalled and tried to protest, but Sven insisted that the division was the way he wanted it.

The weather stayed perfect, and my sons adored the river and the lovely, long, light summer nights. But then, at the end of the week, a message for us from Stavanger was run in to the nearest farm upriver that had a telephone, Finnebu still being mercifully unmodernized. Urgent business called us back to town immediately. There was only one boat a day leaving Årdal for Stavanger, and that would be going in a few hours. Nils Kirkehus had been sick abed for a week, so that was out, and to make matters worse, it was Sunday. On Sunday no God-fearing self-respecting Norwegian peasant goes anywhere except — if he lives near enough — to church. We were much too far from the Årdal church for anyone from the surrounding farms to be going down there, so there was no chance of getting a ride that way. On Sundays the hard-working peasants just sat, in their black clothes, and kept the Sabbath so

strictly that you couldn't even go and pay the milk bill! Money
was not allowed to change hands on Sunday, no matter what
the circumstances.

Since my husband was looking desperate, I offered to go and
see if Sven, who had acquired a farm cart with movable seats
in it, would take us down. But I wasn't hopeful.

I found Sven leaning over the stone wall in front of his house,
chewing a long straw and contemplating the foaming river as
it rushed away under the old wooden bridge.

"Mor'n', Tutti," he said, still looking at the bridge. "Any day
now I expect to see the bridge go, the underpinnings are that
rotten. I've told them down in Årdal, but all they do is promise to come and look at it when they have time." He sighed.

"Sven . . . listen to me . . . I've come to ask a big favor of
you. We have to leave right away, and could you possibly drive
us down to the boat? It's terribly important, and Nils Kirkehus
is sick, and of course my husband will pay you well for your
trouble, and there's no one else to drive us . . . and we have
to get back to Stavanger . . . so I said I'd ask you . . ." My
voice trailed off weakly as I sensed defeat from the expression
on his face.

"Don't see how I could," he answered, looking down at the
ground. You must have forgotten . . . it's Sunday."

"Yes, I know, but please, just this once — couldn't you do it?
We just have to catch that boat."

No answer from Sven, who still stood looking down at the
shoe that he was now scuffing about in the dust. I could tell
from what I could see of his face that some sort of battle was
going on inside of him, and knew him well enough to realize
that nothing more I said would either change or hurry the
ultimate decision. So I too stood there, silently scuffing the
toe of my shoe in the dusty road.

Finally he raised his head, and looking straight at me, his pale face flushing slightly, said, "All right, Tutti, I wouldn't do it for anyone else in this world, but I'll do it for you for old friendship's sake. But tell your husband I will not take any money for it." And with that he turned and went off to the barn to hitch up the horse.

And so we caught the boat back to town, and left shortly afterwards for our home in America. I said goodbye to Sven on the dock, looking at the eyes in the impassive face that betrayed no feeling of any kind, shook the diffidently extended hand, not knowing when I would come again to Årdal.

"Goodbye then, Tutti." He turned back to his cart and drove off even before we were on the boat.

Funny. In all the years that I'd known him, Sven had never expressed himself to me as personally as that morning.

Birkeli

AND SO THE NEXT YEAR, the summer I was thirteen, we came back to Årdal, but to a different house. Nils Kirkehus met us at the dock as usual, drove us up the familiar road, but as we came up the last hill onto that high plateau where you caught your first glimpse of the lake, there, way off in the distance, where there had been nothing but birchwoods, we could see a house, its newly peeled log walls catching the light of the afternoon sun. Ten minutes farther on, the Stolkjerre turned off to the left, onto a new dirt road. Here the horse had to slow down to a walk, as the road was both narrow and rutted from the spring rains. We were all thrown to one side as the wheel of the cart bounced off a ridge of dried mud, then back again as the other wheel hit a hollow; Grandfather and I decided to walk. A wooden gate in a low stone wall barred the way, and once through that we were on Uncle Harald's land. The road wound uphill now, heather and birch bordering it on either side. Off to the right, down in a little hollow, lay a peat bog, blue and white flowers growing out of its grassy tufts.

"Mosquitoes!" said Mother, looking critically at the black ooze between the grasses.

Later on I came to love the little marsh, but at first I used to give it a wide berth during my solitary explorations of the new terrain, as I had heard all too many stories about man and beast being sucked down into that black muck. Little by little I discovered the delights of jumping from tuft to tuft; once I missed my footing, my left leg going down into the spongy black bog, over my ankle. My foot said "shmuck!" as I pulled it out, leaving my sneaker behind. After that I was more careful.

Purple heather grew over much of this moorland and was especially thick around the edge of the bog. It was pleasantly springy to walk on, bouncing back up again after being trodden flat. Once in a while you would come upon a sprig of pure white heather among the purple; this was supposed to bring good luck, like a four-leaf clover.

All sorts of things grew in the marsh that you didn't find anywhere else. There were waving tufts of silky white "marsh wool," that cotton-grass inhabitant of northern bogs, perfect for lining a box to bed down a small doll. There were tiny bright blue flowers on stiff green stems, their five flat petals eagerly turned up toward any ray of sun they could catch.

And there were a few — very few — plants of that rare and absolutely matchless berry that grows only in northern lands: Multer, called bakeapple or cloudberry in English. The cloudberry, so aptly named, for it grows best in the very high mountain marshes, is hard to get to and hard to find, its yellow berries ripening in late summer, hidden under the bronzy-green leaves of its trailing vine. It is our caviar, among all Nordic berries, not to be compared in taste to any other. While it looks like an amber-colored raspberry, it tastes nothing like it, for it has a pungent flavor, sharp and piquant, and many hard little seeds, so that it is one of those berries you crush against the roof of your mouth, rather than bite into.

One of our favorite dinners late in the summer after bird-

shooting had begun, was Braised Partridge sitting on a piece of †
toast richly spread with foie gras, surrounded by small roast
potatoes. This, followed by a dessert of fresh cloudberries and †
whipped cream, was a meal to remember.

"So this is Birkeli," said Mother, still sitting in the carriage
and looking at the house, while Nils Kirkehus and the maids
carried the luggage in.

"Not as large as I would have thought from Harald's descrip-
tion. But then, he often does exaggerate."

Birkeli was an authentic copy of a seventeenth-century Norwegian house, copied from one in the National Folk Museum.
It had two stories of carefully selected logs with the bark peeled
off, sitting atop a good, modern cement cellar. The rather
square, plain look of the house was relieved by a red-painted
front door, topped by a fancifully carved lintel.

This was a house primarily built for people who wanted to
fish; there was ample space and all the equipment necessary
for salmon-fishing, but very few concessions had been made
to feminine desires or taste. Perhaps that was one of the reasons
Uncle Harald's visits to Birkeli were always marked by heated
arguments between him and my mother.

The living room was large and square and was used for
dining as well. It had a long wooden country table, with the
wax and patina of ages rubbed into it. Twelve high-backed
chairs of the same mellow wood came from an old abbey
nearby, recently torn down.

There was one good-sized window, with many small leaded
windowpanes. Unfortunately Uncle Harald and his architect
had found it expedient to make a faithful copy of that old
house in the Folk Museum, and had even refused to adapt themselves to the building site. Therefore, anyone looking out the
living-room window saw a bare stretch of gravel-covered earth,

ending in a clump of stunted birch trees. The long living-room
wall that faced directly toward the lake and the mountains and
the sunset had no window at all.

Mother was in a fury! How stupid could two men be? Her
blue eyes blazed, and she looked as if she would like to push
the whole house over into the lake.

But this was one battle Mother never won. The house was
a perfect example of a seventeenth-century country house, said
Uncle Harald, and he was damned if he was going to spoil
it for anyone's whim. Picture window indeed!

After the first summer, Mother made the best of it, and hung
a large, gaily-colored tapestry on the offending wall.

With all the waterpower from the river, electricity was
easily installed at Birkeli. This made life much more comfortable in many respects than at Finnebu. Not only was there
plenty of light to read by, but the kitchen had a fine big
electric stove, and the bathroom (which had been placed in
the cellar as the only spot, I suppose, that wouldn't intrude on
our seventeenth-century atmosphere) had an enormous electri-
cally heated water tank, so there was no end of hot water for
baths after a damp, bone-chilling day on the river.

There was a lovely smell of fresh wood when you entered
the bedrooms, for the walls had not been treated in any way,
simply smoothed off, the natural wood left to mellow with
time. I was enchanted with my own bedroom, which had two
beds running the length of one wall, encased, like two little
rooms within the larger one, by the joint footboard that ran
to the ceiling and a carved wooden frieze connecting it all
overhead.

Sometimes I would wake in the morning to the sound of cold
driving rain against the windowpanes. The gulls circling the

little island in the lake made a mournful counterpoint of song.
I would snuggle down again into the voluminous bedding that
surrounded and overwhelmed me: the two great square pillows, their linen cases edged with a ruffle of embroidery from
Bestemor's deft hands, and the dyne, that feather-light eiderdown, like a great mound of whipped cream, contained by its
white linen casing. I decided to develop a slight cold — not
bad enough to leave me incapacitated should the sun come out,
or anyone decide to go on a picnic or a drive down to the
general store in Årdal — but enough of one to give me a valid
excuse for spending the day in my little "house." Some careless
guest had left a trashy novel behind, and I wanted to finish it
before it was discovered hidden under the bedclothes. I also
had my box of watercolors on the table beside me. Plenty to
do if left to myself.

Karen would play along with me and send Sigrid up to my
room with delectable morsels for a pseudo-invalid: a mid-
morning cup of tea and a slice of freshly baked Julebrød or a †
cup of delicate Chicken-Lemon Broth; for dinner, perhaps a †
slice of young white veal, sautéed and topped by a butterball †
rolled in chopped parsley.

On the few occasions that I was really ill, a bowl of Fløiels-
grøt (Velvet Pudding) was all I would get. Each country has †
its cure-all for an upset stomach. In Italy it's pasta, plain and
unadorned. In France, a little boiled rice. Well, in Norway it's
Velvet Pudding, no more nor less than a very thick cream
sauce, cooked to the consistency of porridge. The stigma is
partially removed from this starchy mass by serving it sprinkled
with cinnamon and sugar, and pouring over the whole a thin
red fruit sauce. This may not help the stomach much, but the
aesthetic senses respond far better, and who is to say wherein
lies the cure?

Karen was so pleased with her new electric stove, after the old one at Finnebu where she had to chop up the wood before she could even start her fire, that we were in danger of being overfed, and the large oven encouraged continual baking. She baked regularly, twice a week, and among my happier recollections is the memory of waking in the morning to the fragrance of bread in the oven. The delectable smell came drifting up the staircase to my room, and I lay there contemplating the gastronomical pleasure before me, and timing my dressing so that I arrived at the table simultaneously with Sigrid, who carried the round straw basket, its snowy napkin enfolding the

† freshly baked rolls. As I passed the kitchen, Karen was bringing the last of the round loaves out of the oven. They lay, brown and crusty, still steaming slightly as though panting from their recent decalescent exertions. Too fresh to be cut into yet, they would sit and gather themselves until properly matured by dinnertime. There are few things that leave one with a more personal sense of peace and well-being than the sight of one's own fresh-baked bread on the table.

After I was grown up, I lived for one summer in a small village in the South of France. There was a baker who baked all the bread for the village in a large stone oven in the basement of his house. He allowed me, once or twice, to come and watch him as he removed the crusty brown loaves from the oven with a long-handled wooden paddle.

"What do you do to the bread to get such a delicious thick crust?" I asked him, hoping to learn a secret I could apply at home.

"Oh, it's very easy, Madame," he replied. "The first six or eight loaves you put in the oven make the necessary steam to form the crust. You throw those away, and then put all your other loaves in to bake. Et voilà!"

Hardly practical for home baking, but we get around this not only by brushing our loaves with a mixture of whole egg and a little cream, beaten together, but also by placing a pie tin full of water on the oven rack below the bread.

Karen made a delicious oatmeal bread, not from the quick- †
cooking oatmeal in common use for breakfast cereal, but from coarser Scottish- or Irish-cut oats, something one finds quite easily in the U.S.A. too.

My father sent to Norway from Philadelphia, each summer, a large wooden crate of American specialties that my grand-parents were fond of: a couple of fine smoked Virginia hams, tins of California fruit and white asparagus, rated a great luxury in Norway and saved for special occasions. Once he in-cluded a bag of yellow cornmeal, and Karen evolved several recipes out of her head. One, a thin crisp cornbread, became †
such a success that ever after we made our cornbread this way, home in America, too.

She also used the cornmeal for a form of Gnocchi, a very †
good dish for large parties of the help-yourself sort. I use this often with a baked ham, hot or cold, and a mixed green salad.

The hams were large and smoky and were used down to the last small scraps scraped from the bone and put into omelets. †
And the bone itself was used not only for pea soup, but as a base for a magnificent filling Lentil Soup, lavishly laced with †
red wine.

There was, too, Ham and Vegetable Stew, a form of Lob- †
scouse made with carrots and turnips and a handful of fresh peas added to the cut-up ham, a quick and easy dish, popular not only in our family, but among many friends we have served it to in the United States. It also freezes well, and is a handy dish to bring out when unexpected guests drop in, es-

pecially as it can always be extended by adding more vegetables to it.

Then there were all the delectable little cookies and cakes to be served with after-dinner coffee, for in Norway this was a must. There was a loaf of almond-flavored pound cake, called
† Karen's Best Visit Cake, no doubt from the fact that whenever a guest loomed on the horizon she could whip it together very quickly, and have it ready to serve with a cup of tea or a glass of port wine, the minute the (supposedly starving) guest stepped in the front door. There was a cake redolent of
† cardamom, that favorite spice of Norwegians, and a glorious
† sponge cake, *never* to be touched by a knife, but the pieces gently to be pulled off the whole with a silver fork. And little
† Linser Cakes with lemon curd filling.

The first time Uncle Harald came to Birkeli, I begged to be allowed to run up the Owner's Pennant, which could only be hoisted on the flagpole when he was there. This was a grand, oblong, swallow-tailed pennant with his company insignia: a Chinese dragon emblazoned in yellow on a green field, its wicked tongue forking out at you as it waved in the breeze.

It was my job to raise and lower the flags every day, but this time, in my excitement, I forgot to fasten the two ends of the line together, and the dragon sailed neatly to the top, with no way of bringing him down again. Since there was a strict rule about flags being lowered as soon as the sun sank behind the mountain opposite, I was in a panic. I confided my mishap to Sigrid, but at that moment the carriage was seen arriving with Uncle Harald, and everyone rushed out to greet him.

As the sun began to sink, so did my heart, and I could hardly
† do justice to Karen's beautiful dinner: Fresh pea soup, Veal

Paprikash (see page 187) with yellow chanterelle mushrooms I †
had picked in the woods that morning, and for dessert a Four
Species Tart, filled with big white tinned American peaches.   †

The grown-ups were all too busy eating and skåling away,
to notice anything going on outdoors, but I kept glancing at
the window apprehensively, watching the sun just beginning
to sink to the top of the mountain. Suddenly someone came
around the corner of the house, keeping close to the outside
walls, then made a dash over to the flagpole. It was Hans
Bergeland! I had quite forgotten that when I went down to
the boathouse that afternoon, I found Sigrid and that young
Hans from Årdal village, sitting there. He was one of the
linesmen from the electric company, and had helped put in the
wiring at Birkeli, but Grandfather finally ordered him off the
place as he said he spent more time fooling around with Sigrid
than doing his work. I guess he must have stopped in to see
her on his way home from some job in the neighborhood and
found her bathing in the lake, for when I walked into the boathouse that afternoon, she was sitting there in her white cotton
shift, her hair looking all tumbled and damp.

How lucky for me that he was still there, for now, quick as a
flash, he went up the far side of the pole, sure-footed as a cat,
with his climbing spurs digging firmly into the wood. In a
minute he reached the top and brought my fugitive flag and
line down with him, firmly knotted the two ends of the rope
together, folded the flag, placed it over the porch railing, and
stole back to the kitchen wing. I didn't dare look at Sigrid
who was just passing the meat for the second time.

"Whatever is the matter with you?" said Mother, suddenly,
and everyone at the table turned and looked at me. "You've
been sitting there all through the meal without saying a word,
and now you give such a sigh you almost blow the candles

out, and jump when I speak to you! If you can't behave like
a grown-up you'd better go outdoors and make yourself useful
taking down the flag!"

"Yes, Mother — I'm sorry. Please may I be excused? Takk
for maten, Grandmother. The wine was delicious, Uncle
Harald." Having said all the proper things, I vanished out the
porch door, then circled back around the house to the kitchen.
I must thank Sigrid's Hans.

But Karen and Sigrid were quite alone in the kitchen, beginning to wash up the dinner things.

"Oh how wonderful of Hans," I began. "I must thank him,
Sigrid."

"Whatever are you talking about?" Sigrid cut in crossly, as
Karen gave her a quick look, and silly Martha, who was sitting
on the kitchen stoop scrubbing the pots, started to giggle.
"After what your grandfather said to him, Hans doesn't dare
set foot on the place. I haven't seen him for ages."

I started to open my mouth again, then thought better of it.
If Sigrid didn't want anyone to know that Hans had been at
the boathouse this afternoon, I guess that was her business. Most
likely he just happened to be passing by, and since she knew
Grandfather didn't approve of him, she was trying to keep
Hans from getting into trouble. I decided to let well enough
alone.

The large, heavy rowboat that sat in the boathouse was built
in the style of old Viking longboats. It had a high bow, and
attached to this was a piece of flat board that the local boat-
builder had carved into the semblance of a dragon. It was a
far cry from its ancestors, and managed to look more like an
eager puppy than a dragon as it went lumbering across the lake

on the rare occasions that we took it out. Not only was the boat very heavy to row, but it had two sets of long solid wooden oars, that you set into upright thole pins, placed at least ten inches apart, so that the oars slipped and slid around when you pulled on them. If this was what the Vikings had, I don't know how they got anywhere!

Since the boat only took up part of the boathouse, the rest of it was used for washing and drying the laundry. Sigrid and Martha, the extra girl who came to us every day from one of the farms at the end of the lake, soaked the clothes in round wooden tubs filled with water that they heated on a little black iron stove. They pounded and swished the clothes about with wooden paddles and lots of gooey greeny-yellow soap, then rinsed them all out in the lake.

The lake was large and long and deep. It was also very silent and lonely. It lay there like a solitary inland sea, encompassed by the steep black mountains. Rarely did a ripple disturb it, enclosed as it was, and it gave a feeling of no life, either in or on it. Once in a great while some peasant fisherman from one of the two farms that bordered its upper, gentler end would try his luck on the water, but there were very few fish in this large lake, and rarely a boat on it. It looked like the natural habitat for a Loch Ness type monster, and indeed there were tales among the peasants of some sort of giant eel or water serpent that had been seen, looping along, down at the farther end of the lake. But that was many years ago.

The high wooded shore on our side of the lake ran along for a couple of miles, then came to a small green valley where the two farms lay, their fields running down to the stony beach. Several old rowboats lay pulled up on the shore, their paint dry and flaking.

Beyond the farms was a darling little half-moon of sandy beach, sheltered by rock knolls on both sides, with a rising grassy meadow directly behind. Often we would stand on our own shore and look across to the little beach. Even on gray days, when all the rest of the countryside lay in shadow, the little sandy beach seemed to be shining in the sun. Unfortunately we couldn't visit it often, as it took an hour to walk around the stony lakeshore to reach it, and almost as long to row the heavy boat straight across.

Some days Karen would pack a picnic for me, and I would set off on foot along the shore, taking one of Grandfather's hunting dogs with me. There was no need for Mother's parting admonition: "Tutti, you must promise not to go swimming alone in the lake." I wouldn't have gone out beyond my knees on a bet. I knew that not far out the lake bottom took a sudden drop, and I had peered over the edge of our boat and seen the great slimy tree trunks rising from the depths like primordial denizens of the deep, ready to grab the unwary person who came within reach.

By the time I arrived at the little beach I had had enough of the water, and leaving my picnic in the shade of a large rock, I would climb the flower-covered hillside that rose steeply behind the beach. I picked bunches of bluebells and daisies, buttercups and sweet white clover, winding their stems about with straws to hold them together, and placed them carefully in a little rain-filled pool in the rocks, to keep my bouquets fresh until I went home. Then Rikki and I would go and peer down a certain crevice, to see if the brown mother ermine was in, or had left her squirming babies alone. Once I stuck an exploratory hand in, and had a small sharp nip for my invasion of their privacy. After that, Rikki would always back

away from the crevice, barking wild warnings to me the minute
he saw something move, down in the hole.

Sometimes I sat on the topmost rock and sang at the top of
my lungs, literally for hours on end. I sang every song I knew
in English, French, Norwegian, and German. Although I
didn't understand a word of German at that time, I sang them
with much feeling, as I had learned them from a sentimental
young German maid who had been with us for a time, until
it was discovered that her sentimental proclivities had got her
pregnant.

The little beach backed up on the farther side right against
the mountains. They rose straight up above me, black and
forbidding. The topmost peaks could rarely be seen from the
beach below, as they were usually hidden by low-hanging
clouds. This beach was literally the end of the road, for just
beyond it was a gigantic rock slide, several hundred yards wide,
starting at the very top of the mountain and tumbling all the
way down to the lake. It was a formidable barrier of rocks in
suspension, and I was sure it was all controlled by trolls. (When
you live in Norway, you are constantly surrounded by trolls!)

A few goats clambered among the rocks, nibbling at the
tufts of grass that had sprung up among the boulders, but they
never touched the purple foxgloves that grew so profusely. Did
they know the flowers were poison, I wonder?

I was hungry. I took my picnic basket from behind the rock,
sat down, and opened it. In the basket was a small container of
salad, a fresh buttered roll, a handful of dark morello cherries,
and a bottle of my favorite Brus — pineapple flavor.

Today Karen had made for me what she called Chinese
Chicken Salad. There were always a few oriental spices and
foods on our shelves in Norway, sent to us by cousins who had

shipping offices in Shanghai, and Karen liked to experiment with them. The special ingredients can be purchased in most Chinese food shops in the U.S.A.

Visitors came and went that first summer at Birkeli. There was Major B., sitting on the stiff wooden bench outdoors, so well adapted to his ramrod-straight back, gazing popeyed at Mother, like an adoring bulldog. Then Uncle Harald arrived . . . great bustle and fanfare, and Mother now had two admirers, although Major B. was definitely relegated to second place.

And then the Tysons came, with their daughter Poppy. How I looked forward to the arrival of this person I had never seen, who was a girl just my own age. Her father was one of those numerous Norwegian cousins, twice removed, who had gone out to South Africa and settled there. Poppy was an only child, like me, and her parents were bringing her to Norway for a visit. At last I would have a girl my own age to talk to and go fishing and mountain climbing with. I was wild with joy at the prospect. Maybe we would even be allowed to walk all the way up to Nilsebu, that hut up in the mountains that I had never had the courage to walk to alone. We could take some food with us and spend the night! !

The days dragged on endlessly, but finally the day of their arrival rolled round. The Visitors' Pennant was flown from the flagpole, and I hung over the gate outside the house, hours before they could be expected. At last . . . There was the sound of Nils Kirkehus' horse coming clop-clop along the road.

"They're here!" I shrieked at the top of my lungs, as I flung the gate wide open to let the carriage through.

In the carriage sat three people: a tall, thin, dried-up looking old gentleman, a large, plump, elderly lady almost as old as my grandmother, and between them, leaning against the lady, was a pale thin little girl, who made no move to get out of the carriage.

"Poppy dear, we are here at last. Let Mother help you out."

"I'm so tired," came in a fretful voice from the girl.

"Yes, dear, I know. But you can go right up to your bed to rest, and I'm sure your cousin Tutti will be glad to bring you up a glass of milk . . . just heated to take the chill off."

I stared at Poppy as she began to untangle those long, very skinny legs, encased in thick white silk stockings, and ending in white buckskin strap slippers. My eyes traveled up over the rather mussed white dress with lace-edged ruffles, and on up to the dead-white face, relieved only by a few large brown freckles. Six sausagelike pitch-black curls topped by a large white bow hung to her shoulders, framing the small white face. She looked like an old-fashioned pen-and-ink sketch.

Now all the grown-ups had arrived on the scene, and everybody was greeting everybody else with the effusion and the falsely gay voices reserved for people you are related to, but don't know very well, and hope you are going to like.

Poppy and I stared at each other. "You're going to sleep in my room with me . . . we have built-in beds . . . come on, I'll show you, and then I'll take you down to the boathouse . . . and there's time to go to Sven's farm before dinner . . ." and I was off at a run, starting up the stairs, two at a time. Poppy trailed slowly after me, grasping the stair rail with one hand, and pulling herself along.

"I'm not supposed to go fast, ever. I have a weak heart," said Poppy, following me into the bedroom and flopping down on a bed.

I stopped short to look at her. "You do? How do you know?"

"I get palpitations. The doctor says I tire very easily, and must always be careful not to overexert myself." This was said with a faintly pleased expression, each word clearly enunciated as though it had been said many times.

"Don't you have to take gym at school?" I asked.

"I don't go to school. I'm an invalid," she replied. "I could never sit at a school desk all day long . . . my spine couldn't stand it."

"I thought it was your *heart?*" I queried.

"I am gen-er-ally de-bil-i-tat-ed," said Poppy, in a slightly reprimanding tone of voice.

That stopped me. I had no idea what it meant, but she must have something awful the matter with her.

"I do my lessons at home with my governess, and Mr. Phillips — he's my tutor — comes to the house to teach me French and drawing."

Poor Poppy, I thought, never able to run and play with other children. But on the other hand, she was lucky not to have to take gym!

"Poppy, dear heart, it's time for your medicine," and in came her large bustling mother, carrying a bottle containing some brown liquid, and a big silver spoon.

"Yes, Mother dear, just put it down. I'll take it right away, as soon as I finish this lemon drop Tutti gave me."

"Now don't forget it. Remember Dr. Bonnell said it might be fatal for you even to omit one dose . . . and what would your poor father and I do if anything happened to you?" And with a sad little shake of her head, that set her jowls jiggling, she left the room.

"Come on, Poppy," I said, slightly uncomfortable in this sickroom atmosphere. "Let's go see what Karen is making for dessert."

There was a delicious smell of cinnamon and nutmeg coming from the oven.

"What are you making, Karen?" I asked. "Can we help?"

"Apple-Crumb Cake, with Custard Sauce," said Karen.   †

"Mm-mm, Karen," I begged, "please let me beat the eggs and
sugar for you."

"You'll only get that long hair of yours into it," said Karen,
handing the bowl and the beater to Poppy. For all her languid
air Poppy managed to whip up a nice frothy sauce, consuming
quite a bit of it, with a dipping finger, while she worked.

Dinner that night was delicious, but a great deal of it went
back to the kitchen. We had a Spinach Timbale and Mush-   †
room Sauce to start with, made with fresh spinach picked that †
morning, the timbale smooth and light as it should be, but
Poppy claimed she didn't like anything with eggs in — said
they made her skin turn yellow — and her parents spent so
much time trying to persuade her to try just a little bit of it
that they scarcely ate anything themselves. Then we had
Karen's simplified version of a fancy French dish called Veal   †
Orloff, with tiny little new string beans. Poppy took one sus-
picious taste, then laid her fork down.

"There are onions in this. I can't eat onions," she declared
flatly. "They make me very ill."

Grandmother, knowing that there was just a little finely-
minced onion buried under lots of other things in the delicious
sauce, quite lost her patience.

"Well, you'll just have to be satisfied with the vegetables then,
Poppy. And I'm afraid you'll have a rather thin time of it
here, as *we* all like a bit of onion to flavor things. It's an important part of certain sauces."

Poppy sulked, but managed to regain her appetite when two
desserts made their appearance. Besides the Apple-Crumb   †

† Cake, there was a Galette, a lovely open tart of cooked blueberries, combined with fresh uncooked raspberries.

Poppy never ate a full meal at table, but was forever demanding "something crispy" or "something spicy" to nibble on. At
the table she would take one quick look at whatever Sigrid was
passing, and say, "Oh, I can't eat that."

Karen, who had a soft heart, made all sorts of special tidbits
† to tempt Poppy's appetite: Anchovy Sticks, crisp on the outside, suddenly strong and salty in the centers. And the same
† pastry was used for little Cheese Turnovers, square in shape
to distinguish them from the anchovy-filled ones. No matter
how much I practiced I could never roll out the delicate pastry
thin enough to suit Karen. She claimed I just didn't have
"pastry hands," cool and deft like hers.

There was a certain amount of activity during the Tysons'
visit, but hardly in the way I had planned. All activity centered around Poppy, who lay about on the living-room sofa,
or on the chaise longue that had been placed outdoors for
her. Her parents hovered about her and scarcely left her side,
and I was sent upstairs a dozen times a day to fetch a shawl
for her shoulders, a small blanket for her feet, a hat to protect
the delicate white complexion . . . her medicines . . . her
smelling salts. (The first time I opened the bottle and took
a big whiff of the contents I nearly knocked myself out!) She
didn't even bestir herself to go to the bathroom for her needs.
At a slight sign from Poppy, her mother would hasten to fetch
the chamber pot, and bring it down, discreetly covered with a
pale pink towel. Then she placed a large folding screen around
Poppy, and, thus shielded from view, Poppy performed, while
the conversation around her was pitched to a higher level.

It was a very long two weeks, and I was utterly bored with
having my own daily activities curtailed. I felt sorry for Poppy,

but really couldn't quite understand her. In the presence of her parents, she seemed to be continually on the point of expiring. And yet, once or twice when we were actually allowed to go for a walk alone together beyond the first gate, she was quite a different person, who walked and climbed fences, picked berries and chattered away like any normal child.

No one was particularly sorry when the Tysons piled into the carriage again, with all their luggage, and left. Poppy probably wasn't the first fake I had ever met, but she was the first one that I recognized.

The following summer we were so numerous going into Birkeli that Nils Kirkehus met us at the Årdal dock with two carriages and two big carts for the luggage. Besides Grandfather and Grandmother, Mother and myself, there were Uncle Thomas from South Africa with his wife and Uncle Frederick, the youngest of Mother's brothers, who had settled in Pittsburgh and done very well for himself in the steel industry. There were also Mr. and Mrs. Clifford of Philadelphia who had just been on a trip to the North Cape. Mother, having met them at several dinner parties in Philadelphia in the course of the past winter, and hearing of their proposed trip to Norway this summer, in a burst of enthusiasm invited them to come to Birkeli. The fact that Mr. Clifford was over six feet of goodlooking man, as well as an ardent fisherman, may have had something to do with it.

We arrived in brilliant sunshine. The maids had gone on two days before to open up the house, the Visitors' Pennant was fluttering in the afternoon breeze, and delicious smells were coming from the kitchen as we entered the front hall. I went into the kitchen and lifted the lid on the big black iron pot, cooking away on the stove. Mm-mm, Chicken Suzanne for †

dinner, and freshly picked sugar peas, the first of the season.
† And for dessert? A glass dish of Caramel Pudding was
standing on the windowsill, cooling in the breeze. I scraped
the bottom of the small iron pan for the last of the burnt sugar.

Mother had been looking forward to Uncle Harald's arrival
too, as she knew the Cliffords would be both entertained and
impressed by him. In his autocratic way, he was very good
company, and lent a certain flamboyant panache to any group
he graced with his presence, and his humor and wit gave a lift
to the conversation, though often at the expense of others. But
at the last minute something had prevented his joining us.

A few days later it was Mr. Clifford's birthday. A beautiful
† Fødselsdagskringle, a kind of sweet bread, studded with raisins
and citron, the whole thing made in the shape of a very large
pretzel, was on the breakfast table for him. This is the traditional Norwegian birthday offering; nobody is going to wait
until evening for a birthday cake! Dinner was to begin with
a good, clear, homemade broth, because the main dish was
rather rich: Fish Mousse with a lobster sauce (see page 247).

"And of course," said Mother, "we will have champagne with
the dessert.

Champagne? Where was the champagne? And where was
the cognac, necessary not only to accompany after-dinner coffee,
† but also to "flambé" the Bananes-en-chemise, Dorothea, thin
pancakes rolled around a succulent filling? A few bottles of
ordinary French wines were in the larder, and beer, consumed
in great quantities after a long day on the river, was stacked by
the case in the cellar along with some bottles of Scotch whisky.
But the fine wines, the champagne, the cognac, and liqueurs
were all in the closet of Uncle Harald's bedroom, and like
Bluebeard, when he was away, he locked the door and took
the key with him.

Mother was furious! Just because Uncle Harald hadn't turned up as expected, Mother was not going to alter her plans for Mr. Clifford's birthday party. Champagne she wanted, and champagne she would have. She had already tried the door handle . . . no hope, it was firmly locked. Then she went outside, around to the back of the house, where she could look up to the closed windows of Uncle Harald's room.

"I'll show him," she said, and sent for Sigrid to bring her the tall ladder. Fortunately, Grandmother and Grandfather were taking their midday nap, and didn't see what she was up to, but the rest of us stood about watching her as she set the ladder up, directly underneath Uncle Harald's window.

"Come on now, Freddie, you go up and just push the window open." Mother could usually talk this brother into doing anything she wished.

"Certainly not," said Freddie, standing his ground for once. "I'm not going to be accused of housebreaking! This is on your own head!"

Knowing better than to ask Uncle Thomas to take part in this, Mother started cautiously up the ladder. She arrived safely at the double window, but all her pushing at the wooden window frame did no good; the two little hooks fastening it on the inside were firmly in place. She was growing angrier and more frustrated by the minute. Besides, she had an audience, and she couldn't let them down. She was holding tightly to the ladder with one hand, and before we realized what she was doing, with her other hand she took off her leather belt, and gave the small windowpane a sharp blow with the heavy silver belt buckle. In another second she put her hand through the broken glass, undid the latch, and scrambled into the room. Two minutes later she was back at the window, triumphantly holding aloft two bottles of Louis Roederer brut champagne.

This time Uncle Freddie did go up the ladder to take them from her.

"You'll pay for this, Ellinor," he said, as she went back for more champagne and the cognac.

"Pooh!" said Mother, climbing back down the ladder. "I'll have Per put in a new pane of glass tomorrow morning, and Harald will never know the difference."

The window was repaired the next day, and just in time, for Uncle Harald, with no warning, arrived early in the afternoon. He was in a fine rollicking humor and regaled the Cliffords with tales of his recent travels and latest big business deals, and the Cliffords were duly impressed.

"I think I'll go up and get out of my traveling clothes," he said presently. It seemed very quiet in the room when he left; everyone was feeling slightly subdued after last night's birthday celebration.

Ten minutes later Uncle Harald came roaring downstairs like a wounded bull.

"Who has been tampering with my room?" he roared. "Someone has been in there."

Grandmother, knowing nothing of what had been going on, started a small defensive, "But Harald, your room is always locked, and you have the key . . ." One look at Mother's face, and she knew who was guilty. And so did Harald. He started across the room toward her bellowing, "Goddammit, Ellinor, you have all the rest of the house to yourself . . ." But before he had finished the sentence, Mother was up and out of her chair and out the front door. She was *not* going to sit there and have Harald reprimand her in front of everyone — this was really too much! Uncle Harald was out the door right after her. We heard Mother screaming as she ran across the rough ground, toward the little wooded hill beyond the house, and saw her white blouse flashing among the gray rocks as she continued her flight upward. Uncle Harald, starting after her, still in his heavy city clothes, had now thrown aside his jacket, and was gradually overtaking her. They disappeared from sight among the birches at the top of the hill, but I could still hear Mother's voice, only now her screams were turning to breathless laughter. Then there was silence.

"My goodness, I hope he doesn't kill her," said Karen, who had been watching it all from the kitchen window.

Sigrid giggled and said, "I don't think he will."

Meals at Birkeli were entirely governed by the hours spent fishing. Morning tea or coffee was brought up to each bedroom fairly early. Then, after a large breakfast downstairs, the fishermen set off with their rods, gaff, net, and boxes of flies, around eleven. The farthest of the three or four pools was not more than twenty minutes' walk through the little birch forest and down the steep hill to the river by a winding dirt road. In the early part of the summer, the hillside was purple with foxgloves. When you came down to level ground again, there was a stretch of stony pasture between the foot of the hill and the river. A small stream meandered through the stones and grass, and the most delicious little wild strawberries grew here. If I had remembered to bring a pail, I would stop and pick some to take home for jam. If I had no container, I would pick them anyway, and string them as I went, on a long straw, the head of the straw keeping them from slipping off the end. Sometimes I would bring several strawfuls home this way to Bestemor. At other times I would eat them off, starting at the top of the straw and working my way down.

Grandfather seemed tireless as he stood for hours casting his line way out into midstream, the flick of the fly landing exactly where he wanted it to. When he was not alone, or if he'd hooked a fish and wanted someone else to have the pleasure of playing it and bringing it in, he would motion to one of the silent persons waiting on the riverbank (nobody dared speak a word within a hundred yards of Grandfather when he was fishing) and handing over his rod to someone else, leave the big rock he was standing on. Often the little group would divide, each going his own way to a separate pool, hoping *he* would be the one to bring a salmon home.

Sometimes dinner was at four, more often nearer five. This was the main meal of the day, but we did not usually have a first course unless guests had just arrived, or it was some special occasion. There was always a hearty main course of whole boiled salmon, or a large roast of veal, lamb, or pork, whatever could be bought from the neighboring farms. If good meat was hard to get in the country, it would be sent in to us by boat from Stavanger. I don't remember having beef very often: I imagine it must have been difficult to get it there in the mountains.

But, ah, those succulent little chickens! Karen cooked them in a variety of ways: there was Chicken Suzanne (see page 217), party food, and fairly elaborate, but a favorite with all of † us. Sometimes we had Chicken Sebastiano, the little birds simply split in half, and baked in the oven while being continually basted with a mixture of oil, lemon juice, and herbs. And when Karen had no idea when the fishermen would be † back for dinner, a quick method: the chickens cut into quarters, seared in a pan, and left to simmer with tomatoes and cream added.

At least two, usually three vegetables, besides the ubiquitous potato, were served with the meat. Butter was not added to † the cooked vegetables, but a separate dish of Rørt Smør (Lemon Butter, see page 257) was often served as accompaniment.

Usually the men went out fishing again in the evening, after eight o'clock, when they claimed the light was just right in certain stretches of the river. They would only fish for an hour or two, coming home, still in the long, light Nordic twilight, to sit on the terrace with a well-earned Scotch-and-soda, or if it had been a cold drizzly day, Grandfather would say, "I think we need a little glass of Snaps." (Aquavit.) Sigrid would bring the thimble-sized glasses and the bottle of fiery white liquor. There is a very old saying about this drink that seems appropriate:

"The Aqua Vitae is comonly called the mistresse of all medycynes, for it easeth the dysseases comyng of cold. It giveth also corage in a person, and cawseth them to have a good memory and remembrance when it is dronke by reason and measure."

I've never known it to help my memory, but a small glass or two of Aquavit does warm and cheer one more quickly than any other drink I can think of.

By ten, the table would be set for supper with all kinds of cold dishes — meats, salads, sardines, salami, cheese — and usually one hot dish, kept warm on a *réchaud*.

Since it was easy to get tender young veal in the country, and we were so numerous, we usually bought an entire milk-fed calf at the beginning of the summer, and had the farmer butcher it for us. So we ate a great deal of veal, and also enjoyed the fringe benefits of liver, kidneys, and even sweetbreads, which Karen looked at askance, but made into an incomparable supper dish with ham, mushrooms, and a sherry sauce.   †

A Swiss recipe for veal kidneys was a particular favorite of †
Grandmother's and gave her a chance to show off her culinary skill. After Karen had assembled the ingredients for this dish in the kitchen, Grandmother did the finishing touches herself at the table in a chafing dish. She particularly liked setting

fire to the brandy and swirling the kidneys around in the flaming sauce, then dishing it out, still burning bluely, as though she had made the whole dish herself for each and every person she served.

† Sometimes for supper there were hot cheese ramekins, little cheese tarts made of flaky pastry, filled with a hot cheese custard, and baked a delicate brown. Other times there was large, † shell-shaped macaroni, stuffed and baked with tomato sauce. Both my grandparents had traveled on the Continent in their younger days, and their sons had also gone far afield; everyone brought back one or two new dishes each time he came home, to swell Grandmother's recipe file. One dish — its country of † origin unknown to me — had a strange name, Kolkauna. It made a hearty supper dish on days when we had had only a light dinner. A round platter was heaped high with mashed potatoes, pieces of boiled onions mixed all through it. This was surrounded by Middagspølse, a veal and beef sausage, cut into slanted slices, and put together again to form a whole. I use this quite often at home in America for Sunday night supper, served with a green salad. Although the Middagspølse can be ordered from some Scandinavian delicatessens, I use a variety of sausages, and find this dish very good with the small American breakfast sausages that can be bought anywhere. A tasty, filling, easily prepared, and inexpensive dish.

There was never any dessert at supper; it was a pleasant, leisurely meal, served informally, with people passing the various dishes on the table to each other. Sometimes beer, but usually hot tea, was served at this meal.

Shortly after the Cliffords left, the weather turned gray and drizzly. Doors stuck, Karen's lovely bread grew moldy, and the kitchen stove and living-room fireplace were continually festooned with drying clothes. The smell of mildew and damp wool pervaded the air. Uncle Harald went off on a business trip, and Mother decided she was not going to spend the entire summer fishing, but would go off to London to have some fun with friends there.

So the big Vuitton trunk was packed and sent ahead to Claridge's, and Grandmother, Grandfather, and I were left alone. The atmosphere was rather peaceful and relaxed for a change. Grandfather took me fishing with him, and even let me gaff a small salmon for him one evening, all by myself.

Karen let me help her in the kitchen. We made a delectable dessert from a recipe that Gustava, our party cook in Stavanger, had given her: Krokankrem, a cold Praline Whip, studded † with toasted almonds. (This is a marvelous summer dessert and can be made ahead of time. It also freezes well and can be kept for future use.)

Two weeks passed and then word came from Mother that she was back in Norway. She and Uncle Freddie were in Oslo, and were going out to Hankø for the Royal Regatta. There was to be a big ball at the end of the week; the King and Queen would be present, and also the Crown Prince who was sailing his own six-meter boat in the Regatta.

Mother came home a week later and told us all about the wonderful time she had had at Hankø, and that the Crown Prince had danced with her twice at the ball. It all sounded very glamorous, and I immediately visualized Mother dancing with a golden crown on her head.

It was the first of August, and the weather had turned beautiful, which was fortunate as the Matsens were about to arrive. Like the Tysons, they, too, were from Cape Town, and were relatives of Grandmother's. After my experience with Poppy, the previous summer, the fact that they were bringing with them their two daughters stirred me not at all. I had a mental picture of all South African girls as being wan and weary.

This time I was wrong. Sylvia, six months older than I, was bright, imaginative, and as full of mischief as a monkey. She was built like a skinny young boy, and her freckled snub nose and short-cut blond hair added to the impression. I took her upstairs to my room.

"What kind of school do you go to over there in America?" she asked, and before I could answer her she went on, "I go to a convent. The nuns smell like mice, they never wash, and *we* have to take baths with our nightgowns on. I lifted mine once when Sister Veronica came in, and, ooh, did she scream! I had to say ten Hail Marys as punishment."

"Oh," I said, "I go to a Quaker school. We have to go to Meeting for *hours* every Thursday and just *sit*. Nobody says a word." It sounded very tame compared to Sylvia's convent. "Are you a Catholic?"

"Not really," replied Sylvia. "I was sent there when I was twelve for being caught in the greenhouse with the gardener's son. Wow, did my Dad beat me!"

I was intrigued and was on the point of asking, "What were you doing?" but thought better of it. The punishment made more of an impression on me than the unknown crime. No one had ever laid a hand on me harshly, although I was always being sent to my room as punishment for something.

"How old is your sister?" I asked. In contrast to Sylvia, her sister was most feminine and romantic looking. She wore a wide-brimmed straw hat with a long pastel-colored chiffon scarf that started at the crown, floated gracefully over the brim, and ended wound around her slim neck. I was open-mouthed with admiration.

"Irene? Oh she's *old*. Nineteen. And she's *hopeless*. She's in love and just sits around mooning and waiting for letters."

"Is she going to get married?" I asked, always so prosaically romantic.

"Not to *that* one. Father brought her on this trip to break it up. He's an Afrikaner."

"You mean he's *black*?" I asked, absolutely fascinated.

"No, of course not, silly. Just *Afrikaner*. And, after all, Mother is English."

"Oh." I was not much wiser, since African mores were not as widely publicized in those days.

Poor Irene, she must have had a rather thin time of it at Birkeli. Sylvia and I were much too young to be of any use to her as companions, the rest of the family too old. She spent a great part of the day sitting alone on the white wooden bench in front of the house, polishing her lovely long nails with a little cake of rouge powder and a chamois-skin buffer, and waiting for Nils Kirkehus to arrive with the mail.

Though I had all sorts of projects that kept me busy when I was by myself, for loneliness engenders invention, they were not as physically strenuous as the things Sylvia thought of. By the end of the second day she had explored every nook and cranny, every rock and hillock in the immediate vicinity of Birkeli. I had also taken her to Sven's farm, where she distinguished herself by climbing onto the highest rafter in the barn, and with a wild African tribal yell, jumping off into the hay, so far below that neither Sven nor I had ever dared try it.

One lovely sunny morning I woke to find Sylvia looking at me with that puckered brow and slightly quizzical look that meant she was dreaming up some new adventure for the day, and wondered if I would go along with it.

"Let's go and have breakfast. I've got an idea!" And she jumped out of bed, pulled on a pair of underpants and a faded cotton blouse and skirt, stuck her bands on her teeth, and was out of the room while I was still washing my face.

I came down to the table to find her taking some of the freshly baked rolls out of the bread basket, and stuffing them down the front of her blouse.

"Whatever are you doing that for?" I asked, as I helped myself to the scrambled eggs Sigrid had just set down.

"Ouch! They're hot!" said Sylvia, pulling the neck of her blouse out, and blowing down her front. "Take some cherries."

I obediently stuffed a big handful of cherries inside the front of my yellow blouse, where a red stain began rapidly spreading.

"Matches," said Sylvia, picking them up from the ashtray. "Hurry, or the others will be coming down for breakfast. We'll need a frying pan and something to cook, but how can we get them while Karen's in the kitchen?"

Blindly following Sylvia's lead, not knowing where we were going, but excited at the thought of an adventure, I suggested going by the outside cellar door to the extra food larder down in the basement. Some sliced bacon, a discarded frying pan, and a bottle of fruit juice were added to our supplies. We piled it all into an empty vegetable basket, and set off along the lake shore, in the direction of the river.

"It's silly to live indoors in weather like this," announced Sylvia. "At home in South Africa I often sleep outdoors in a tent, out on the veldt."

"Alone?" I asked.

"Well, no," she answered, "Father usually sends one or two of our Kaffirs to sleep outside the tent, in case of animals.

There's nothing to be scared of here. Your grandfather told me that there are no wild animals here, not even monkeys. Isn't that funny?"

I would have thought it funnier if there had been monkeys among the birch trees in Årdal, but of course it all depended on your point of view.

"Let's go climb the hill on the other side of the river," I suggested. "There's a big flat rock up on top we can sit on, and cook."

"And sleep on," said Sylvia, bent on a life in the open.

It was a very warm day, and having crossed over the old wooden bridge, we decided to go and cool our feet in the river before tackling the hill, which looked more like a mountain, from where we sat at the foot of it. We went on steppingstones to a big rock, almost out in the middle of the river, and having removed our sneakers, sat down and dangled our feet until they tingled from the icy water, and felt quite numb. We were entirely alone, with woods and rocks and river all to ourselves.

"We'd be much more comfortable climbing the hill without our clothes on — it's so hot," said I, having none of Sylvia's convent-bred inhibitions about nudity. "But we'd better put our sneakers back on," I added. "There's a sort of a little path, and it's quite stony."

We took off our clothes and left them on the rock, and I picked up the basket and led the way up the hill. We started off at a brisk pace, sometimes following the little trail, at other times leaving it to climb over moss-covered rocks, enjoying the feeling of alternate hot sun and cool shadows on our naked bodies as we wound upwards among the birch trees. We climbed silently for about twenty minutes, then Sylvia offered to take the basket, and we threw ourselves down on the ground in a little open glade, to take a breather.

Far below us was the river, foaming whitely as it went its winding way down the broad grassy valley. We could see almost the entire length of it, as it wound around Old Svein's fields, down past Forkpool, the dividing island looking like a small overgrown rock from here, down to Sandpool, almost out of sight. In the opposite direction we could see where the river began, surging out of the lake through a narrow gap. Our eyes followed the shore of the lake, around to our boathouse. Was that Sigrid rinsing out clothes down there? How lovely and free we felt up here by ourselves, with no clothes on, and nobody to tell us what to do and what not to do. Look! There were Mother and Grandmother out for a walk on the path along the river. Good thing we knew they wouldn't come climbing up here. Now they were crossing the bridge, stopping to look at the swirling water below. Mother was gesticulating toward the water, and even from way up here I could tell how excited she was. She turned toward Grandmother, then started to run back toward Birkeli, leaving Grandmother to follow more slowly.

"Probably saw a salmon, and has gone back to get her rod," said Sylvia. "You know how twitchy they get over fish. I'm hungry! Let's go on up to your rock and cook something."

We climbed on up, and as we arrived at the top, turned for another look at the river. Why were there suddenly so many people on the bridge? And wasn't that Uncle Freddie talking to Old Svein way down near the bend of the river on the opposite side? Feeling that we were missing something, we nevertheless turned our backs on the scene below, and set about starting a fire in the lee of the big rock. We were not very successful, as the wood refused to catch, so we finally decided to leave the bacon for the birds, and ate the rolls, the squashed cherries, and drank the tepid fruit juice. Not a very satisfactory

meal, even though we found a few blackberries to supple-
ment it.

Some clouds were hiding the sun, and a cool little afternoon
breeze had sprung up. Perhaps we should at least have kept a
shirt to put on . . . I was still hungry, and tried to remember
what Karen was making for dinner that night. Was it veal
chops in a casserole, with all the finely chopped vegetables mak- †
ing that succulent mush? And Swiss Potatoes, crisp, and redo- †
lent of cheese? I knew she was making a Strawberry Soufflé for †
dessert.

I felt a pang at the thought of all this good food we were
missing. Maybe it would be better to go home, and come back
tomorrow with blankets . . . and more food! I started to suggest this, hesitantly, to Sylvia, who was sitting hunched together
hugging her knees, her teeth chattering between faintly blue
lips. She was up on her feet and on her way down the path
almost before I finished speaking. There was no one in sight
below us, and we made straight for the rock where we had left
our clothes. They were not there.

"The dirty dogs! Who do you suppose stole them?" Sylvia
exploded.

Our teeth really chattering now, we crept back home, going
around through the birch woods and squish-squash through the
little marsh, as we suddenly felt too naked to walk in the open
along the lake. We arrived at Birkeli, and for some minutes
stood behind a clump of bushes, waiting to see that the coast
was clear, then made a dash for the open door, and quickly up
the stairs to our room. How nice and warm a sweater felt, and
my blue flannel slacks. Perhaps no one had missed us, and we
could just pretend we had been to see Sven. I hoped Mother
wouldn't ask me where my red skirt and my yellow blouse
were.

We walked downstairs, and, our two faces set in expressions of studied innocence, strolled out onto the terrace, where all the grown-ups were sitting, talking in somber tones. The pall that hung over the assembled group lasted only until our families saw us. If we had dropped a bomb in their midst, the reaction could hardly have been more violent. Mother, with a shriek, bounded across the terrace and tried vainly to gather me into a maternal embrace, but since I was almost as tall as she, and there was too much of me to gather up and take on her lap, she ended by clinging to *me* for support, and sobbing loudly, "My baby! My baby! I thought you were dead!" I began to think that my poor dear Mother had quite lost her mind.

Sylvia's father, on the other hand, reacted quite differently to the return of his erring daughter. Holding her firmly with one hand, he undid his heavy leather belt, and turning her over his knee, beat poor Sylvia so hard that they must have heard her shrieks all the way down in Årdal. As the leather belt swished through the air, landing with regular thuds on Sylvia's bottom, her mother sat in a chair nearby, sobbing into a tiny lace-bordered handkerchief, her ample bosom heaving at each thud. The thought passed through my mind that this man must settle everything by beatings. Maybe that was the South African way.

Grandmother, during all this, calmly went on with her knitting. After all, she had raised seven children. She looked over her knitting at Mother, and said, "I told you they would turn up, Ellinor. I wish you had more than one child, you wouldn't worry so."

Grandfather had long since firmly settled his spectacles on his nose, and gone off to look at the raspberry bushes.

And now our parents, having relieved their pent-up emo-

tions, dispatched us, supperless, to bed. A kind Sigrid sneaked
up with some bread and cheese and milk for us, and an expla-
nation of what had gone on that day.

It had all been a matter of bad timing. If unkind fate hadn't
sent a little breeze along to blow our clothes off the rock, and
into the river, just at the moment that Mother and Grandmother came along on their walk, no one would have been the
wiser about our expedition, and we would now be downstairs
eating a good dinner, instead of being locked up here. Mother
had caught a glimpse of my red skirt, and Sylvia's faded plaids,
swirling downstream past Old Svein's fields. Prone to instant
panic, she decided that we had been swept down the river
(whether *in* or *out* of our clothes, she never did stop to reason).
What made it more alarming was that the only piece of clothing left on the rock was my yellow blouse, with a big red stain
from the cherries, just below where my heart would have been
. . . if I'd been in it! This was tangible proof to my imaginative mother that I had been murdered (or worse!) before my
body had been flung into the water.

Sylvia and I were house-bound for two whole days, only
allowed to come down for meals, and then sent upstairs again
to separate rooms. That wasn't too bad, as the rooms were ad-
joining, and we worked up a nice code by rapping on the wall
between us.

The enforced inactivity only served to stimulate Sylvia's pro-
pensity for getting us into trouble. For two days after we were
let out of captivity, we were absolutely angelic and did all
the proper things expected of us. We shelled peas for Karen
for pea soup and for Risi-Bisi to be eaten later in the week. †
Karen well knew that our willingness to help in the kitchen

wouldn't last long, so she took advantage of our services while she could.

We willingly ran errands to Old Svein's farm to fetch the eggs and the milk, carrying the heavy milk container home without dawdling on the way. We picked pailfuls of blue-
† berries for Blabaergrøt and Blueberry Tarts, we dug around in the springy moss under the birch trees for the lovely orange-colored chanterelle mushrooms. I sat for what seemed hours, holding skeins of yarn for Grandmother, while she wound it into a big ball for the afghan she was crocheting, while Sylvia polished her father's high brown laced boots till she could see her freckled little face mirrored in them. Altogether our behavior was exemplary for two whole days.

The morning of the third day Sylvia and I stood on the up-stairs porch, looking out at the lake.

"Let's go down to the boathouse," said Sylvia. "We could row over to that little island and explore."

"You know we are forbidden to take the rowboat out on the lake alone," I intoned virtuously. "They say it's much too tippy and we don't swim well enough."

We went down to the lake anyway. In the boathouse were two round wooden tubs that Sigrid and Martha used for washing clothes. The fact that the washtubs were ten times as tippy as the rowboat didn't stop us for a minute, and we were soon on our way to the island, each of us paddling her own little washtub, legs dangling over the edge, roaring with laughter at the effort of going in a straight line without turning turtle.

Suddenly there were shouts from the house, and two minutes later Sylvia's father and Uncle Freddie were gesticulating and calling to us from the beach. There was no mistaking the words that came across the water to us. "Come-home-imme-diately."

"Damn," said Sylvia, as we reluctantly changed our course. Two more days of confinement to our rooms, but by now we had our Morse code perfected.

Summer was almost over, and Mother decided to leave Birkeli the following week and join the Matsens in Oslo for a few days before we went our separate ways: they, the long trip back to Cape Town, Mother and I, home to my father in Philadelphia.

The Grand Hotel in Oslo is almost as much of an institution as the Royal Palace, which is situated at the opposite end of the same wide street. One feels they almost have a nodding acquaintance with each other. Our bedroom at the Grand was enormous, and the two beds were set back in an alcove, draped in voluminous red damask. The beds, too, were outsize, and boasted three large pillows each, and a huge fluffy eiderdown quilt. A long gold-framed mirror, of the sort called a pier glass, reached from floor to ceiling, between the lace-curtained French windows that opened out onto a balcony. The balcony railing was festooned with hanging pots of bright pink begonias and trailing ivy.

Sylvia and I were on our own and were supposed to amuse ourselves — with definite restrictions on our activities — without interfering with our parents' social engagements about town. Hotel life for children can be very confining, and they did not think we were old enough to wander about town alone, so it took a certain amount of ingenuity to while away the hours while we were waiting for them to come back to the hotel and spring us loose. We used up all the Grand Hotel stationery we could lay our hands on, to make paper darts which we aimed from a second floor corridor down on the unsuspecting heads

of people sitting in the Palm Court below. A hit counted two points, but a direct strike on a bald head got you five. When we ran out of writing paper, we turned to other diversions. We discovered a wonderful pastry shop directly across from the side entrance of the hotel, where we could sneak out without being caught. We spent all our pocket money there and would weave back across the street, dodging traffic as we carried our boxes
† of cream puffs, cakes, and cookies back into the hotel. Up the many flights of back stairs we would go, to the huge hotel attic, where we crouched in a dark corner, hidden by rows of hotel linen hanging to dry. Here we sat and stuffed ourselves without interruption.

I was just finishing my third raspberry tart, when Sylvia, swallowing the last bit of cream puff, looked up above her and said, "I wonder if that skylight will open?"

The next moment Sylvia, from the top of a stool set on a table, had the skylight open and was halfway out of it.

"Come on," she said, as her legs disappeared through the opening, "there are things on the roof to hold on to."

I have never been one for heights, in fact I think twice before mounting a ladder, but in the past month I had blindly followed where Sylvia led, so up I went too, and out onto the steep slope of slippery blue tiles. She was already halfway up to the ridgepole, where the three-foot letters ꓶƎTOH ꓷИΛЯꓨ loomed above us. Perhaps it was her South African background that made Sylvia as agile as a monkey on the roof, while I climbed shakily after her, carefully placing each foot, and clutching the evenly spaced iron handles for dear life. Halfway up I knocked a tile loose with my foot and heard it go bouncing down the roof, and, much later, fall with a shattering sound into the back courtyard of the hotel, seven floors below. My stomach gave a sickening lurch.

"Come on, silly," said Sylvia, "before you knock the whole roof down!"

I finally made it to the top and stood with Sylvia on the narrow ledge of the ridgepole, clutching the big letters for support, and peering down at the busy street and the park below us. I was beginning to feel more at ease up there, and began to point out the familiar sights of Oslo to Sylvia. Seen from this new vantage point they suddenly took on a more entrancing air.

"Look at that little island out in the harbor. That's The Queen restaurant, and there's the Royal Yacht Club with all the sailboats around it. Look! There's one of the square-rigger training ships in from Sweden." I waved excitedly, slightly intoxicated at having successfully negotiated the steep roof.

"I know," Sylvia answered. "I saw a couple of the cadets in town yesterday. They're cute! I wonder if . . ." But I was never to know what Sylvia wondered, for at this moment we both looked down at the park and saw, directly opposite us, a small knot of people all craning their necks up in our direction, and in their midst — there was no mistaking the elegant figure in the blue dress and the large hat — was Mother, now beckoning wildly to us, and turning appealingly to the young man accompanying her as though she expected him to fly through the air immediately and retrieve us for her.

"Uh-oh — trouble . . ." said Sylvia, and started down the roof backwards. I followed, just as fast, and far more scared of the anticipated punishment than of the dizzy heights.

The old strap was brought out again (Sylvia must have had calluses on her bottom by now), but I was let off this time with a scolding, since we were all parting the next day, and I guess Mother had run out of punishments by then.

Sylvia and I swore eternal friendship, promised to write frequently, and parted most reluctantly. Two days later I was quite happy to be on the boat, homeward bound, even though it did mean going back to school.

It also meant getting back for that lovely late-summer season of American lima beans and American corn on the cob, and homemade peach ice cream, and the wonderful Peach Meringue Cake that our American cook constantly made for my father. Home, there, had its attractions too.

To Paradisnes – and Back Again

THE FIRST THING I remember about Tante Kirsten is her beautiful slim pointed shoes. They were pale cream-colored kidskin, with high heels, and they were absolutely immaculate — not a scratch or a smudge anywhere on them.

Mother and I had just arrived at the big house in the country outside Bergen, to visit her old friend, Kirsten Thorsen. It was early summer. This was the first of many visits to a house that is as vivid in my childhood memories as that of my grandparents.

It was late in the evening; I was four years old, and tired of traveling all day from Stavanger. It was way past my bedtime, though it was still a lovely light evening.

I stood in the big front doorway, neither in nor out, shifting tiredly from one foot to the other, while Mother and Tante Kirsten greeted each other delightedly and immediately tried to catch up on all the gossip of the past year, quite oblivious of me in their pleasure at seeing each other again.

Finally, in a desperate bid for attention, "What's that big mountain over there?" came from me, as I pointed across the fjord.

"Why, that's Ulrikken," said Tante Kirsten, turning and looking at me for the first time.

"I want to climb up it. Now!" I stated firmly, and I turned and started out the door again.

Tante Kirsten laughed and bent down and took me by the hand. At this moment I made another discovery. She had very dark, soft hair, and she smelled absolutely delicious.

"You don't want to go up Ulrikken tonight," she said. "We'll do that tomorrow. But now, let's go see what Lina-cook is making for us in the kitchen."

I was torn with indecision, but the kitchen seemed nearer than the mountain, and she still held my hand. I turned and walked alongside the trim, pointed shoes as they click-clacked across the black-and-white marble floor of the hall.

Lina-cook (who was always designated thus, to distinguish her from "Old Lina," the chambermaid), was fat and blond, with a smudge of flour across the end of her nose. She was making something that looked like a miniature tower out of a lot of little brown pastry puffs. I watched as she dipped each puff into a shiny brown syrup and carefully placed it on top of the round half-built construction, like someone building a fairy-
† tale castle. It was called a Gâteau St. Honoré.

Tante Kirsten picked up one of the small puffs lying on the pastry board, and said, "Open your mouth and close your eyes." My mouth was suddenly filled with something sweet and creamy, and thus, unable to protest, I was led away to bed.

The house was large and square and painted white, with a mansard roof of shiny blue tiles. It sat on a slight rise on a beautiful point of land that extended out into the fjord. The house had many rooms, and was surrounded by well-cared-for lawns and gardens. There was a large garage, with a big black limousine, and a small Renault town car, and in the apartment above lived Bjørklund, the ill-tempered Sweedish chauffeur.

He spent his days washing and polishing the cars, always buttoned up in his high-collared uniform, waiting for orders.

At the foot of the garden was the bathhouse, its roof supported by four white marble mermaids standing on their tails, looking out over the fjord. Mornings that we swam, a maid appeared at the bathhouse at the stroke of noon, carrying a silver tray with a bottle of champagne in a cooler, fruit juice for the children, and a platter of thin sandwiches.

There was a tennis court, and a velvety green croquet lawn, and a greenhouse full of flowers and clusters of dark blue grapes hanging from carefully tended vines.

In the garden was a small pool, with lotus plants sent from China, and by its edge stood a bronze statue by a famous French sculptor.

This was about as close to heaven as one could get in Norway.

Inside the house, the rooms were large and airy, windows opening on all sides to the garden, and the surrounding fjord. There was a library with a large desk at which Uncle Magnus transacted much of his business. He spent a great deal of time pleading loudly with the telephone Frøken to please put him through to his office in town. He was a broad, tall man, and the decibels of his thundering voice rose to such a peak that he could quite easily have been heard in town without benefit of wires.

The house had a "French salon," used mostly for evening parties, with carved French chairs, covered in pale pink silk damask, and a grand piano, and paintings by the best Scandinavian artists of the time, and four large portraits of the four girls of the family done by an excellent postimpressionist. For there were four daughters in the house; in fact this was the only way in which Tante Kirsten had failed her husband; he had no son to carry on his business, only a house full of women.

Perhaps that is why he sounded so loud and angry much of the time. It was his way of asserting his independence and masculinity. Still, his shouting never frightened me, for I discovered at an early age that beneath all the bluster was a kind heart, a good deal of humor, and great love for all his females.

Next to the salon was the room we generally sat in in the evening and on days when it was too rainy to be outdoors. It was the Peisestue, the Fireplace Room. It had large comfortable chairs and a sofa with soft cushions that you sank into, all covered in a silky plum-covered velvet. There were tubs of purple gloxinias to match the room, just as there were huge chased-brass tubs of begonias in the pink salon. There were always great bowls of fresh-cut flowers in all the rooms. I have only to get a whiff of stock at some florist's today to recall vividly that lovely mixed fragrance of wax-polished floors and vases of thick creamy-white stock that pervaded the whole house.

Beyond the Peisestue was the dining room. There was a long oak refectory table in the center of the room, to match the English wall paneling, and the service plates on the table were of heavy hammered silver. There was usually a large silver bowl filled with roses in the center of the table, although Uncle Magnus always protested, saying that the scent of flowers detracted from the taste of the food and wine.

Tante Kirsten was the first person I ever knew who, in those days of the standard white damask tablecloth, had the imagination to use color on her table. The damasks were dyed lovely shades of pale peach, or soft green, and for special dinners she would use as a tablecloth a length of silver and green Italian brocade. For really grand occasions, when diplomats and VIPs from Italy came to dine — for Uncle Magnus was honorary Italian consul, among other things — a great length of cut vel-

vet, red with an underlying pattern of old gold, was laid on.
I remember seeing the table once, set with this rich red cloth,
the silver plates reflecting the soft candlelight, and in the center
of the table a huge oval silver platter, heaped high with small
scarlet crayfish, providing a feast for the eyes as well as the first
course.

Everything in the house was pleasing to the eye and to the
senses. There was very little food for the mind. Few books
were read, and the piano was rarely played. In fact, the only
music I can remember in that house is the Marlene Dietrich
records that Lillemor and I played, much later, when we were
growing up, over and over again on a small portable record
player, as we sat on the floor in the front hall: "Jo-o-o-hnny,
wenn du geburtstag hast . . . Bin ich bei dir zu gast . . . die
ganze na-a-cht . . ." We tried to emulate the sultry voice, half
in love with the unknown Johnny ourselves, and feeling terribly
wicked at the intimation in that phrase, "die ganze nacht" —
"the — whole — night!"

Everyone in the family was fluent in several languages, had
beautiful manners and impeccable taste. But very little of im-
port stirred. The conversation stayed close to personal prob-
lems and crises, and the gossip of the town.

Tante Kirsten ran the house expertly, with the help of four
efficient maids. Apart from the six members of the family,
there were often visitors from abroad, like us, visitors who
came, not for a short weekend as we do nowadays, but for two
or three weeks, or even as long as a month. Anyone who had
embarked on the rough trip across the North Sea, or spent the
better part of a week coming by train from Italy, was going to
stay for a bit to make it all worthwhile. In a way it was easier
on the hostess, who felt no compulsion to cram a lot of entertainment for her guests into a few brief days. Instead, the guests

were simply absorbed into the family life, which made it much more relaxing for everyone. No particular fuss was made over them, once they had arrived and were settled in their own quarters, and they came and went as they pleased. There was a good-sized guesthouse out beyond the croquet lawn, and a maid who had entire charge of it, preparing the guests' morning tea there, pressing their clothes, and seeing to their comfort.

The grown-ups spent their days sitting on the flower-planted terrace looking out over the fjord. Here they chatted endlessly about their friends, of visits to London and Paris, or of their last trip to Baden-Baden to take the waters. They drank tea and coffee, fruit juice or champagne with graceful indolence, and the smoke from the fat Turkish cigarettes especially made for them on the island of Cyprus floated slowly upward in the clear Nordic air.

Visitors came to call, and also sat endlessly on the terrace. Dinner was a movable feast, so a brief call often lasted three or four hours. No one was ever in a hurry, everything was here, why go somewhere else? Once in a while one took a stroll through the gardens, or to the greenhouse to see if the grapes were ripening, or played a leisurely game of croquet.

Those were lovely days of dolce far niente, all very soothing like a thick, velvety fog. And time stood still there, all during my childhood and the growing-up years. Then the Germans marched in and took over, and everything changed for the family as it did for everyone else, in so many different ways. But that was much later.

Of the four girls, three of them had the black hair and dark eyes of their mother, and looked like anything but the traditional Norwegian. Even Ellin, the only nonbrunette, was only blond by contrast. I think that in the small West Coast town that Tante Kirsten originally came from, some marauding Spaniards, strayed north from the Armada, must have left a strong strain of Latin blood in the veins of the coastal Norwegians! (I don't think I'm making this up.)

Margit, the eldest, was already an elegant young lady fresh from boarding school in England when she came into my life, so that my first memory is of a very slim, dark girl, sitting on the terrace steps, twisting the long string of pearls her father had just brought her, between the fingers of one hand. A young man sat next to her, one of a series, undistinguishable from the rest, his blond head very close to her dark one, as he whispered in her ear. Her long slim legs were continually crossing and uncrossing, like a restless colt who wants to go somewhere, but isn't quite sure where.

Though they were surrounded with all the luxuries of life, Tante Kirsten trained her daughters to run a house well, in the only way that really counts — by making them learn how to do the things themselves that they would later, in their own houses, direct others to do for them. Margit's specialty was the making of what we now call cocktail canapés, or hors d'oeuvres. This was all before the invention of the cocktail per se, but in the long hour before midafternoon dinner, people drank a glass of dry sherry, or Madeira. Margit would come proudly in from the kitchen, bearing a tray of delectable tidbits, not only delicious to the taste, but pretty to look at. There were little canapés of pâté covered by aspic — a wine aspic — and made in †
the tiniest of tart shells, salvaged from the dollhouse in the attic. There were hot Curried Chicken Balls, a small mouthful †
each, with a crunchy outer coating, and Délices d'Emmental, a †

† melting, cheesy confection. There were Hors d'Oeuvres Anna, little rounds of toast heaped high with a wonderful combination of grated cheese, white of egg, and a secret ingredient that gave it its tantalizing what-is-it? flavor.

One day she brought in a round little pat of cheese, with a coating of chopped nuts. It was absolutely memorable, spread on crackers.

"What in the world have you made this time, Margit?" asked Tante Kirsten.

"Oh, I just found some odds and ends of cheese in the larder, and I mushed them up together — with some other things — " and here she laughed, for no good cook likes to give away all her secrets! "And there were some chopped nuts that Lina-cook

† was going to use for a cake, so I rolled my Cheese Ball in those."

All four daughters learned to cook, and with the exception of Lillemor, whose talents lay in other directions, they were all expert in the kitchen.

† Most memorable of all was the Caviar Roulade conceived by Ellin, the second daughter. Ellin was the mournful one, always entangled in the endless complications of some long-drawn-out love affair with no possible solution. One day, to distract herself, she decided to experiment with the fresh caviar that arrived at Paradisnes by boat from Russia, once or twice a month, packed in metal tins surrounded by ice. She came up with a long roll filled with caviar and sour cream. Uncle Magnus protested vigorously at this desecration of good caviar, until he tasted it. From then on, the roulade took its place as a favorite first course.

Since in those days in Norway, and in that family, the finest caviar was easily come by and taken for granted, it was sometimes mixed with other ingredients and made into a spread.

While I do try to make the roulade with pressed black caviar (which is excellent for this dish, and half the price of the fresh), I make a very good spread with the much less expensive red caviar (salmon roe), which blends well and has an attractive † color.

Lillemor and I, being the same age, shared a bedroom. Actually, the room belonged to Lillemor and Astrid, the youngest, but while I was there Astrid was sent to sleep in the little room next to the English governess. Astrid, an adorable roly-poly creature and her father's pet, was too young at that time to be a part of our lives.

I remember particularly the long closet that ran the length of the room. From a metal rod, about twenty feet long, were suspended dozens of little dresses in pairs, each pair in two different sizes — for Lillemor and Astrid were always dressed alike — and all in different light colors. On a rack underneath was a long line of well-polished shoes, black patent, red leather, white buckskin, and sturdy brown oxfords for walking. This was Lillemor and Astrid's wardrobe, ordered twice a year from Paris. Most of the dresses were made with the skirt hanging loosely from a short yoke, appliqued in white linen, or delicately embroidered with flowers. Their skirts were much shorter than my American ones, for this was the way little French girls wore their dresses. When they ran, their skirts flounced around and showed their lace-edged panties. We all wore the same kind of white cotton panties, edged with a shirred ruffle of coarse Irish lace, set on an openwork band.

We all had long hair hanging down our backs. It got into dreadful snarls and tangles by the end of the day, but in the morning we came down to breakfast with neat long sausage curls that Missy had painstakingly brushed, one by one, over her long bony forefinger. Before going to bed, we were prepared for the next day by having our hair rolled up on thick cotton rags called Pappelotter. They made our nights miserable, as there was always one bumpy roll pressing on a nerve somewhere, and an injudicious turn on the pillow woke you right out of a sound sleep. What tortures we suffered for fleeting beauty!

When we were quite young, the only boys Lillemor and I came in contact with were the ones brought to Paradisnes by friends of our parents. They looked uncomfortable in their blue serge suits, and there was little communication between us while at the dinner table. Once outdoors, after dinner, while the grown-ups lingered over coffee, things went a bit better. We played croquet, or, evading the gardener's watchful eye, stole grapes from the greenhouse. Once in a while some enterprising little boy, finding himself alone on an isolated garden bench with one of us, would sneak a tentative hand up under our skirts, but the tight band of Irish lace effectually stopped this juvenile experimentation. Since the panties were buttoned firmly to a sturdy linen "panty-waist," we were practically impregnable. Did our mothers plan it that way?

By the time we were fourteen or fifteen, boys would sometimes come out from town to see us. I guess part of the attraction was the fact that I was Lillemor's friend from America, and they wanted to practice their schoolboy English. We usually retired to the hall, and with the record player going full tilt, proceeded to dance the tango around and around the room. We would turn, and swoop, and go into deep dips, our partners bending us far backwards in the best Rudolph Valentino tradition.

It was all quite dull, and the only men I ever hankered after were the older ones who came to see Margit and Ellin, but they, of course, never looked in my direction.

In an era when people sat about a great deal of the time, meals were an important part of the day. Strangely enough, with all the delicious dishes that came out of the kitchen at Paradisnes, only the cook was fat. Perhaps it was due to the fact that there was only one big main meal a day, which was rare at that time. Also, there was very little hard liquor drunk, although when there were visitors, the men usually had a Scotch-and-soda before retiring at night.

Meals were not only well executed by Lina-cook, but well planned by Tante Kirsten. If a meal started out with a rich first course, such as the Caviar Roulade, or that lovely extravagance of Tante Kirsten's made of ham and artichoke bottoms, † foie gras, and Madeira Sauce, the following course was necessarily a simple and sauceless one. On the other hand, if the first course consisted of a bit of homemade pâté on a lettuce † leaf, some Beet Soup, or Lina-cook's inimitable Cheese Snaps, † a more solid course would follow — perhaps, Breast of Chicken † with white asparagus, the whole blended by a lovely rich sauce.

In a country where the freshest of fish was always available, we sometimes had plain grilled fillets of sole, served with a Pink † Sauce, a recipe someone had brought from Sicily. Or Fish Mousse, with a shrimp or a lobster sauce, or fillets of fish baked † in a sauce with shrimps, oysters, or whatever shellfish was in the market that day. Sometimes this was varied by using crab † with it, the fillets of fish on the bottom of the dish, and a layer of crab meat on top. Except for the Fish Mousse, which takes a little more time and care in preparation, all these dishes are simple and easily made. And even the Fish Mousse, with the help of our modern blenders, doesn't take too long. In my childhood the cook had to scrape all the raw fish, painstakingly, by hand.

An American friend who married a Norwegian once told me that, as a bride, she decided one day to cook something for her husband from the Norwegian cookbook her mother-in-law had given her. She opened the cookbook at random, and the first recipe she saw, graphically illustrated, began, "Take one calf's head and split it in two . . ." My friend hastily closed the book and placed it on the top shelf, where it has been ever since.

Fortunately we have found ways of getting around chores like that, or simply eliminating them. For that strangely marvelous fish-and-meat dish called Forloren Skilpadde (Mock Turtle Stew), we simply substitute nice little pieces of veal for that awful head. At least I do!

In the fall there were ptarmigan, still softly brown-feathered, heaped high on the kitchen table. A richly moist dark-meated game bird, it was roasted whole in an iron pot, a little stock and sour cream added at the end of cooking, and a small amount of that brown Norwegian goat cheese added for flavor. Sounds strange, doesn't it? A famous French chef once told me that he adds a tiny bit of Roquefort to ptarmigan, or sauces accompanying strongly-flavored game.

One day, when we were alone at Paradisnes, just the family and no guests, Ellin came bursting in with news from the kitchen. "We're going to have the most wonderful thing for dinner today! Sprengt Oksebryst!"

Everybody in the family seemed to be unable to wait for this extraordinary dish, and dinner was advanced from four o'clock, to three.

"Why, it's just Corned Beef and Cabbage," I exclaimed in deep disappointment, as it was set down on the table. It turned out to be a very good salted brisket of beef, served, not just with cabbage, but with various vegetables, small and fresh from the garden.

Rice, as a starch, was not used much in Norway as accompaniment to fish or meat. Most of the time there were boiled potatoes with chopped parsley or a sprig of dill decorating them. The potatoes were always fluffy and mealy, never soggy, and I think this comes from the fact that after all the water was poured off them, the cook held the lid over the pot and gently shook the potatoes for a minute, being careful not to break them.

On the occasions when we children did overeat, unable to resist a second helping of "Overturned Applecake," smothered † in whipped cream, or took a third little pot of delicate flowered Rosenthal china filled with smooth Mocha Cream, we would † get up from the table groaning that we were V.M., which stood for Vemelig Mett, a forbidden expression denoting fullness to the puking point! If we were overheard, there would be only thin tea and a dry wafer for us at suppertime, in order to teach us to control our appetites in the future.

I think I suddenly began to grow up the summer I was fifteen. When I came to Paradisnes that year, I felt like a very different person from the summer before, when Lillemor and I were content just to row on the fjord, fishing for mackerel, or dig for little gray shrimps in the slippery seaweed down in the cove. Mother had given me one or two of her discarded dresses, and I was allowed to put my hair up in the evenings. It made all the difference in the world and I felt very grown-up. Lillemor's conversations about the boys she had met at dances in Bergen during the winter began to bore me. I had met a lot of boys at dances in Philadelphia, too. In fact one of them

had sent me a leather-bound volume of love poems by a then
popular and very sentimental poetess, Sara Teasdale.

"He sent it to the boat when we left America," I told Lillemor. "He also sent me some big purple orchids. Mother
wouldn't let me wear them. I suppose she thinks I'm not old
enough!"

Lillemor was impressed by the orchids. "Is he in love with
you?"

"I suppose so," I answered diffidently. "He does all my math
papers for me in school."

Mother was off on a round of visits again, leaving me with
the Thorsens. I felt quite at home there, but this year, for some
reason, I was restless and bored with the pleasant, uneventful
life at Paradisnes. But the peaceful rhythm of life was suddenly disrupted the day Uncle Magnus came home from his
office and announced that the Italian Crown Prince and his
entourage were arriving in Bergen the following week. And
of course, since Uncle Magnus had an honorary position with
the Italian government, His Royal Highness would have to be
entertained at Paradisnes.

"His Royal Highness is only going to be in Bergen for two
days," Uncle Magnus informed us. "He is on his way north
to fish the Alta River." Uncle Magnus started off for his wine
cellar.

"By the way," he said, turning at the door, "the Prince is
traveling incognito."

Incognito! A real royal prince! I began to take an interest
in life again. I knew it would be a large elegant dinner, for
this was the kind of thing the Thorsens' life had trained them
for, if for nothing else. It put them on their mettle, and everyone was immediately galvanized into action. Lillemor and I
were set to polishing all the antique pewter and the big brass

and copper flower containers in the entrance hall. Ellin was dispatched to the greenhouse to see what flowers were coming into bloom, and Astrid was sternly ordered to keep Bonzo, her beloved boxer puppy, out of the house, from now on. Tante Kirsten went to consult with Lina-cook about the menu, and the necessity of having extra help for serving. Did Lina think Bjørklund could be depended on to wear his white serving gloves, and to serve the wines properly without drinking up half of them in the pantry? Lina-cook assured her that all would be taken care of, and she would keep an eye on Bjørklund herself. Lina was one of those supercooks who like being put to the test. She would get quite depressed if there were no guests and she only had us children to cook for.

Uncle Magnus reappeared from the cellar, carefully carrying several cobwebby bottles.

"It's a good thing I've been saving that Bernkasteler Doktor, '21," he murmured to himself. "It will go well with the fish. And if we have beef, this fine old Romanée-Conti, 1906, should be superb."

(I shuddered reminiscently. At my first big Thorsen dinner party, the year I was thirteen, I had timidly asked for a little water to dilute my wine. There was a horrified silence that spread around the table. "Spoil my Romanée-Conti!" thundered Uncle Magnus. "Give Miss Tutti some fruit juice and water until she is old enough to appreciate a good wine." I was mortified, and tried desperately to hide my face in the glass of fruit juice that the maid brought me.)

"Fortunately one of my ships just brought me in several cases of Louis Roederer brut champagne. Dee-licious! Dry enough to dry the baby's diapers!"

"Really, Magnus," protested Tante Kirsten, "please don't repeat that for His Royal Highness's benefit!"

Margit, who had just become engaged, flew to the grand piano in the French salon, and swept into a Strauss waltz with great vigor and many mistakes.

"Silly," said Lillemor, passing through the room with me, "you don't really think you're going to be allowed to bore that poor Prince with your piano-playing, do you? Besides, you always play a B-flat instead of A-flat in that middle passage." Lillemor marched over to the piano and firmly pounded A-flat several times.

"Beast!" said Margit, flouncing off the piano stool, and went to find her mother. We heard her say, in her most wheedling voice, "Don't you really think we must have some music for the Prince, Mother?" and Tante Kirsten's kind but firm answer, "No, I really don't, Margit. Dinner will be long, and after that you know the men always like to sit over their coffee and cognac. I don't suppose His Royal Highness is any different from them in this respect." Margit sulked for days.

However, she quite made up for it when the Prince arrived. The Prince was all that he should be: tall, dark, and handsome, and in his late twenties. Margit, in her low-cut evening gown, didn't have to play the piano to attract his attention. Instead, she volunteered to show him the garden while we all waited for after-dinner coffee to be served in the French salon. There was absolutely no hesitation on the part of His Royal Highness. Before anyone could think of creating a diversion, Margit slipped out the side-terrace door, the Prince following closely after. We saw her long white chiffon dress go floating off in the direction of the boathouse.

By the time they returned, the coffee was quite cold, the Prince had a slight smudge of lipstick on his white shirt collar, and Margit's fiancé was seething. Tante Kirsten immediately started an animated conversation with the Prince's aide, and everyone followed her lead, prattling on about nothing in that well-bred way, all the while wondering what had really taken place.

The dinner itself had gone well. Bjørklund wore his white gloves, and served the wines without a tremor, and the Prince, who had taken the trouble to learn the rather rigid rules of skåling in Scandinavia, lifted his wine glass to each lady in turn, gazing at them over the rim of his glass with his large brown eyes, and enchanting them all. In each case he held the glass just a shade too long.

I kept one of the gilt-edged menus, written in Tante Kirsten's fine slanted handwriting.

MENU

Consommé Double, au Madère

Filets de Sole, Bonne-Maman

Filet de Boeuf, Ecossais

Legumes Printanière, Hollandaise

Canard Farci, Maison

Salade d'Endives de Brussels

Poires, Son Altesse

Mother came back to Paradisnes two days later, quite cross at having missed all the excitement. We were still recovering from the effect of the Royal Visit. The leftovers of that grand dinner having been finished the day before, we were on simple rations for the rest of the week: Lina-cook's own version of Potage Santé (Health Soup) followed by plain roast veal.   †

Mother did not arrive back at Paradisnes unaccompanied, but brought with her Benedict, a cousin from north of Oslo, a great lusty man whose primary interest in life was hunting and fishing, and Jacob S., a friend with the same tastes. She

was taking them in to Årdal with us for the last salmon-fishing
of the season, and it was time to pack up our clothes and say
goodbye to Grandmother and Grandfather, before we set sail
for America. Jacob's younger brother, whom Mother had not
yet met, was also to join us at Birkeli. I looked forward to
being back in Årdal.

It was nice to be at Birkeli again, and Årdal was having
lovely end-of-summer weather. Grandfather and Grandmother
were happy to have us back, and welcomed Benedict and Jacob
warmly, too. My hair was down my back again in two pigtails, and it was a relief not to have all those hairpins sticking
into the back of my head. I dug out a couple of old cotton
dresses from the closet. They were too short, and rather tight
across the bosom, but still, I felt at ease and was comfortable
in them. Maybe I didn't want to be grown-up yet, or at least
only on occasion.

I had been off to the little sand beach around the other side
of the lake, and came into the living room. I had quite forgotten that Jacob's brother was arriving. He was sitting by the
corner fireplace, and Mother was just bringing him a tall
Scotch-and-soda.

"Oh, Tutti," she said, turning and seeing me as I stood
hesitating in the middle of the room. "This is Jacob's brother,
Oluf. Did you find any wild raspberries over by the beach?
Karen needs them for a sauce she is making."

I stood — rooted — in the center of the room. He was sitting
in the old wicker chair near the fire, half turned away from
me. I took a quick look at the handsome profile, marred only
by a slightly weak chin. Then I noticed his hands. I had never
before thought about a man's hands being beautiful, but these

were long and slender with smooth, well-cared-for, square-cut fingernails. The backs of his hands were brown, as though they had recently been exposed to the sun, and the fingers gave an impression of controlled strength, and at the same time, great gentleness. He was pulling together the strings of a small leather tobacco pouch, and a straight-stemmed pipe was in his mouth. He turned around with a rather lazy movement, to look at me, then got to his feet. He was very tall and blond, and his blue eyes had those thick light brown lashes that one often sees accentuating a Norwegian face.

He had a very relaxed look, due in part to the half-closed sleepy-looking eyes, and the ease and animal grace with which he moved. He was twenty-six years old. The eyes of the opposite sex had been telling him for some time now, that he was a very attractive man.

I took one good long look at him, stammered, "How d-do you do, Velkommen to Birkeli," and fled to the kitchen with my basket of raspberries. My knees were trembling, and my heart thumping so that my ears buzzed, and I felt quite dizzy. I leaned against the hall wall for a moment, then walked into the kitchen and put the basket down on the table.

"Here are your raspberries, Karen," I said. "There aren't very many left."

Mother was used to picking and choosing when it came to a question of whose attentions she would accept. And she could be quite cruel to the "discards." There was a young Russian, on one of our trips across the Atlantic, who sat on the footrest of Mother's steamer chair, looking at her with the hungry expression of a great shaggy dog. Now and then he would timidly address some words to her in his low husky voice. His faulty English and guttural voice must have amused

her, for she smiled when she looked at him, but she never
answered him. Once, I saw her strike him rather sharply
across the cheek with one of her leather gloves. He continued
to sit worshipfully at her feet all the way across the Atlantic.

Now she was in her late thirties, and at the height of her
beauty, but I suppose she felt the forties creeping uncomfortably
close. She began to make some effort to draw the complete
attention of every male who crossed her path, as though to
convince herself that her powers of attraction were as strong
as always.

Oluf was much younger than she was, but he was of her
world, and he had been around, so a matter of a few years
was not going to stand between them. She played a half-
teasing, half-flirtatious game with him, like someone flicking
a piece of string in front of a kitten, then drawing it away as
it grabbed for it. Only Oluf didn't seem to want to play, which
only spurred her on to greater efforts. He seemed perfectly
content, after a season of sailing and partying at Hankø, to go
fishing with the men, or to go for walks alone, or simply to
sit by the fire, smoking his pipe, his nose buried in a book.

To me he was very kind, in his nice lazy way. Sometimes
he walked to Sven's with me to fetch the milk. Other times
when I was sent to get the mail from the box at the end of
the long entrance road, he would say that he needed to stretch
his legs, and come with me. He opened the heavy wooden
gates for me and, laughing at me for being afraid to walk
through the herd of cows that stood directly in our path, cut
a little birch switch and chased them away. I felt protected,
and he became for me a combination of the father I missed,
and the brother I had never had. When we were at table, or
all sitting in the living room, he always included me in the
conversation, addressing me as though I were one of the

adults. For the first time in my life I was entirely happy at Birkeli and had no desire to return to America.

Mother came into the living room dressed to go fishing. "Oluf, do come along down to Sandpool. You're so lazy!" And she walked over to where he sat, and gave a small tweak to his hair.

"I think that pool is about fished out," he answered, smiling up at her as he smoothed down his hair with his hand. "I wouldn't want to take the last fish away from you."

Looking slightly exasperated, Mother left the house, saying, "Don't forget to go and get the cream for dinner, Tutti," and hurried off to catch up with Benedict and Jacob.

I started to go out of the room to fetch the pail.

"Will you come with me, Oluf?" I asked hesitatingly.

"Of course. Are you going now?"

"In a little while. I'll call you," and I went to the kitchen.

"What are we having for dessert, Karen?" I asked, perched on the high kitchen stool. I was just stalling for time; I couldn't have cared less about food at that moment. I was trying to decide what I had in my closet that looked better than this old plaid cotton. More seductive!

"Fruit tarts," replied Karen. "I need the cream for the chicken gravy."

I slipped off the stool and went upstairs to my room. Now where was that low-cut Mexican blouse that someone had brought Mother last year? She said it wasn't her style, and had recently given it to me. There it was, in the back of the closet. I could wear my blue skirt with it. The white blouse was a bit loose for me, and had a tendency to slip off at the shoulder. No matter, I'd keep my shoulders slightly squared. I looked at myself in the small mirror. The lace around the décolleté was definitely becoming against my sunburnt skin.

But, ugh! those pigtails — that would never do. I undid them, and brushed my hair hard to get rid of the crinkles from the tight braids.

"Oluf," I called, as I came downstairs, "let's go." I walked out the front door, swinging the little pail, and feeling slightly self-conscious. I heard Oluf come out behind me, but didn't turn to look at him till he was by my side.

"Mm-mmm," he said, taking in the change in my appearance, "you look very nice." (Is that all? I thought. Why doesn't he tell me I look like a dream? If it were Mother he would. *All* men said things like that to Mother — *always!*)

It was a warm day and we walked slowly through the little birch wood and out onto the dirt road that led to Sven's farm. I was looking for chanterelles as we walked, but it had been a dry summer and there were none to be seen.

"Tutti, do stop walking with your nose to the ground like a bird dog," said Oluf, taking hold of my arm and guiding me firmly among the rocks and overgrown tree stumps. I liked the feeling of his rough tweed jacket against my bare arm.

Sven was out repairing the old stone wall in front of their house.

"Good afternoon, Tutti," he said, looking at the pail I held. "Have you come for cream?" I nodded. He took the pail from me silently and disappeared into the cellar of the house. I picked a few overripe currants from the bushes by the wall.

"Taste!" I said, holding out the handful of berries to Oluf. "They're not sour at all."

He leaned over and put his mouth to my upturned hand, and ate the berries like that. His mouth was warm and moist, and his tongue tickled the palm of my hand, and I found it strangely pleasant. He looked up at me as he ate the last berry, his eyes crinkled and smiling. Was he laughing at me, I wondered?

Sven returned, firmly pressing the lid down on the cream pail.

"If you walk home by the river," he said, as he handed the pail to me, "watch out for the new fence we've put up. It's electrified."

We started back down the road again. I looked at the steep little hill that rose up, right from the river. This was the hill Sylvia and I had climbed, the day our clothes floated away. How silly and young I was just one year ago! This hill was one of my favorite spots, though, and I hadn't been up its slopes at all this summer.

"Would you like to climb up the hill?" I asked Oluf. "You can see the whole river from about halfway up."

I led the way up the steep narrow path. There were some late wild strawberries, and I stopped to pick them as we climbed, and strung them all onto a long straw. We came out from among the stunted birches, to an open space, a small mossy plateau, with a few bluebells growing here and there in the crevices of the rocks. I picked two or three, and holding them up to Oluf's ear, shook them gently.

"Listen," I said, "you can hear them ringing." I stood in front of him, holding the bluebells, looking down below at the river, and swaying back slightly against him. He put his hands lightly on my bare shoulders, and the back of my neck rubbed against the topmost button of his jacket. He was tall, and I felt warm and protected by the sheer physical presence behind me. We stood looking down at the river, winding like a shining silver ribbon in the low rays of the late summer sun.

"You can follow the river all the way down to Sandpool from up here. Isn't it lovely?" I asked, turning to look at him.

"Very lovely," he replied, pulling me down beside him onto the mossy ground. "And so are you," and he kissed me gently behind the ear in a place that made me shiver with delight. I was going through very mixed feelings as I lay there in the sun, happy, excited, and slightly apprehensive, all at the same time. I picked up the string of strawberries, and dangled them above me.

"Wonder how they'd taste dipped in the cream," I said, carefully lowering them into the little pail. I lay back, and holding the dripping string high above my face, started to pull the bottom berries off with my teeth. The cream dribbled in fat drops over my chin and down onto my bare neck.

"Don't you ever think of anything but food?" Oluf asked, and proceeded to lick the cream off my skin, with lingering caresses of his tongue. I had never felt so completely happy in my life, although I was far too young at that moment to realize that the relationship between eating and making love is a very complex thing.

We lay there in the sun, our heads very close together on the moss, eating the strawberries with a sensual slowness. We were there for a long time before picking up the pail and starting down the hill again.

I felt deliciously warm and happy and sure of myself, as though I had added a dimension to my being. Now I knew what I was. A combination of strawberries and cream, sunshine and love, had made me into a woman.

After all, virginity is an entirely relative term.

The Recipes

Stavanger Recipes

Tuna-Bean Salad

1 cup small white dried pea beans or 1 12- to 15-ounce can
1 7-ounce can tuna fish
⅓ cup vinegar
½ cup olive oil
½ cup chopped green pepper
1 cup green onion tops (scallions) cut into small pieces
1 tablespoon chopped parsley

salt and pepper to taste. With dishes containing fish, I use Nepal pepper. It is very hot and must be used sparingly, but gives a unique flavor.

Optional: a few slices onion, chopped fine, or a clove of finely chopped garlic.

Boil the beans following directions on package, until soft but not mushy. Drain well and cool. Put tuna fish into a bowl and break up into small bits with a fork. Add other ingredients to this and mix all gently together with the beans. Chill for at least an hour, and serve as a salad or as a first course.

Roast Pork (Ribbe)

loin of pork, 4 to 5 pounds	1 cup orange juice or 1 cup sherry
2 tablespoons dried rosemary	salt and pepper

Rub the loin of pork with salt and pepper and sprinkle with dried rosemary. Roast in a preheated 350° oven for two hours, basting frequently with orange juice or sherry. Serve the meat cold, very thinly sliced, and accompanied by a compote of dried apricots and prunes.

Lobscouse (Lapskaus), Norwegian-American Line

This is Lapskaus as it is made for the crew on Norwegian ships at sea.

3 parts corned short ribs of beef	onions and leeks
1 part lean corned pork	peppercorns
4 parts raw potatoes	

The beef and pork should stand in water overnight to draw out some of the salt, the water being changed once. Cut the meat and potatoes up into half-inch cubes. Put a good dollop of butter into a large frying pan, and cook the meat in this, browning it slightly. Add the sliced onions, the sliced leeks, and the cubed potatoes. Cook until potatoes are done, stirring

carefully from time to time so as not to make a mush. Grind
whole pepper over it.

This is how I make it for use in my family:

3 pounds corned short ribs of beef	4 tablespoons butter
1 pound lean corned pork	4 large onions
6 large potatoes	6 leeks

Follow instructions as above.

Pyramid Cake (Kransekake), Norwegian-American Line

½ cup sugar	1 tablespoon almond extract
2 egg yolks, hard-boiled	1 cup coarse sugar
2 eggs	a little extra egg white, beaten
1 cup butter	slightly
3½ cups flour	

Mix sugar with the hard-boiled egg yolks. Beat the two whole
eggs with butter, and combine the two egg mixtures. Gradually
sift in the flour, kneading well. Add the almond extract while
mixing. Take a small lump of dough, and roll between the
hands into a finger-thick strip, long enough to form a circle
seven or eight inches in diameter. This is for the bottom ring
of your pyramid. We suggest that you roll out all the strips
first, making each one a little shorter than the one before. Dip
the ends of the strips of dough in the slightly beaten egg
white, and join. Place them separate on several large slightly
floured cooky sheets, sprinkle them with coarse sugar, and bake
in a quick oven until light brown. When removed from the
oven, immediately place one ring on top of the other so that
they will stick together. Decorate.

Icing

> 3 ounces confectioners' sugar   ½ teaspoon lemon juice
> ½ egg white, beaten slightly

Combine ingredients. It is customary to begin decorating by piping a thin line of white glacé icing in zigzag lines all over the cake in an irregular design. Continue decorating with snappers and favors.

Lemon Fromage

> 2 eggs, separated   1 cup cream, whipped stiff
> ½ cup sugar   grated peel of 1 lemon
> 2 tablespoons gelatin, softened in   a little candied lemon peel or
>   ¼ cup cold water   candied lemon slices for garnish
> 2 tablespoons lemon juice

Beat egg yolks and sugar together until light. Dissolve gelatin and lemon juice over hot water. Stir well and cool, but do not allow to stiffen. Whip cream stiff, add grated lemon peel and softened gelatin, and fold in the stiffly beaten whites. Fold into the egg-yolk mixture and pour into a mold. Chill until set, unmold, and garnish with candied lemon slices or candied lemon peel.

Pineapple Fromage

> 2 eggs, separated   1½ tablespoons gelatin, softened
> ¼ cup sugar   in ½ cup pineapple juice
> 1 15-ounce can crushed   1 teaspoon lemon juice
>   pineapple   1 cup cream, whipped

Beat egg yolks and sugar together until light. Add all the

well-drained pineapple except for one tablespoon which you save for garnishing. Dissolve the gelatin with the pineapple juice and the lemon juice over hot water, and cool. Beat egg whites until stiff and fold into egg-yolk and pineapple mixture. Add the melted, cooled gelatin and the whipped cream to this, and stir all well together. Turn into serving bowl and set in refrigerator to chill. Garnish with rest of crushed pineapple, or — prettier — with pineapple wedges.

Rum Omelet

6 eggs	4 tablespoons dark rum
4 tablespoons heavy cream	3 tablespoons butter
3 tablespoons sugar	pinch of salt

Separate eggs, putting yolks in one bowl, whites in another. Beat yolks, adding cream and two tablespoons sugar, one tablespoon rum, and pinch of salt.

Beat whites stiff and fold into yolk mixture. Melt the butter in a medium-sized pan and pour omelet mixture into it. Cook over medium heat, lifting edge of omelet from time to time with a spatula, to see if it is lightly browned underneath. When done, slip from the pan onto a platter, folding it over lightly in half. Just before serving sprinkle with remaining tablespoon sugar, pour over the three tablespoons warmed rum, and set fire to it.

Rice Pancakes (Rislapper)

This is a fine use for leftover boiled rice.

1 egg	1 tablespoon milk
1 tablespoon sugar (scant)	1 cup boiled rice
1 tablespoon flour	1 tablespoon butter

Mix egg and sugar, stirring well until smooth. Add flour, then gradually the milk, continuing to blend. Stir the boiled rice into this. Melt butter in a pan, and when beginning to brown, drop batter by spoonfuls into it, frying like hot cakes until brown, turning them once. Serve with jam or jelly or maple syrup.

Pancakes or Crêpes (Pannekaker)

1 cup all-purpose flour	2 eggs
2 cups milk	1 tablespoon sugar (only for
¼ cup (4 tablespoons) melted	dessert pancakes)
butter	¼ teaspoon salt

Place flour in a bowl and add milk gradually, stirring well, then add other ingredients, beating to eliminate all lumps. I use a wire whisk for this. Let the batter, which should be of the consistency of cream, stand for at least an hour before using. To cook: Heat a small (six to eight-inch) pan good and hot, so butter sizzles when you drop it in, then turn down a little so it won't burn. I always use clarified butter (see below) for this and all other frying or sautéeing. Put a teaspoon of butter in the pan, and swirl it around to coat the pan completely. Pour in about two tablespoons of batter and quickly swirl about to cover bottom of pan evenly. Cook crêpe until edges begin to look dry, and lift a little with a spatula to see if it is brown underneath. Turn, cook for a few seconds on the other side, and remove from pan.

These pancakes can be used in many ways. They can be made ahead of time and reheated, and can be frozen and quickly thawed when that unexpected guest arrives. They can be used for dessert, filling them with jam or jelly, and, omitting the sugar, as a main dish. Stuffed with crab meat, or minced chicken, or almost any leftovers, mixed with a little cream sauce or leftover gravy, then rolled up and put in an ovenproof dish and heated, with a little sour cream on top to blanket them, they are delicious, economical, and impressive when brought to the table.

Clarified Butter

Place butter (I use three-quarters to one pound at a time) in a saucepan over low heat. When butter has melted, skim off surface foam, and then pour off the clear yellow butter into a bowl, discarding the milky white fluid in bottom of saucepan. I keep a small bowl of clarified butter on hand at all times for sautéeing or frying. Food cooks more evenly in it, and does not burn as easily since the impurities have been removed.

Blueberry Pancakes

2 eggs	¼ cup sour cream
1 tablespoon sugar	2 tablespoons melted butter
½ cup flour	¾ cup blueberries
¾ cup milk	

Mix all these ingredients together, and proceed to cook as in recipe for pancakes. Serve with a little powdered sugar sprinkled over.

Fruit Soup (Saftsuppe)

3 to 3½ cups berries (cherries, raspberries, blueberries, gooseberries, or all of them mixed)	2 to 3 tablespoons sugar
	4 to 5 thin, thin slices of lemon
4½ cups water	2 tablespoons potato starch

Remove any stems or leaves remaining on berries, and if cherries are used, pit them. Rinse the berries and put in a pot with the water, sugar, and the lemon slices. Simmer until the fruit is soft. Blend the potato starch with a little cold water, and add this to the berries to thicken the soup a little, stirring all the while. Bring to a boil, then turn off heat immediately. Serve in wide soup plates with a slice of the cooked lemon in each dish.

As a variation, instead of thickening with potato starch, five tablespoons sago (like a very fine tapioca) may be added instead. The sago must boil until it becomes transparent.

This Fruit Soup is delicious cold, as well as hot. When served cold, a spoonful of whipped cream on top is a nice addition.

Wafer Shells (Krumkaker)

Krumkaker are baked in a special iron, resembling a small, thin waffle iron. The iron closes tightly and turns out a thin, quickly-crisp wafer that stiffens almost immediately, so it must be placed in a cup or around a wooden cone right away, to shape it while it is still soft. When served, the wafer shells are filled with whipped cream or berries or preserves.

2 eggs	1 cup milk
1 cup sugar	1½ cups flour
½ cup melted butter	1 teaspoon vanilla

Beat eggs and sugar together until smooth and white. Add melted butter, milk, and flour, stirring until smooth. Add the vanilla. Heat Krumkake iron and when hot (a drop of water on the inside should sizzle), drop about one tablespoon of batter inside the iron. It should fill the inside thinly, but completely. Close top, and bake a very few minutes until light brown, turning the iron once. Remove wafer from iron with a spatula and shape by putting into a teacup, or around a cone, while still hot. Recipe should make about thirty wafers. Keep in a dry place.

May also be filled with following recipe.

Mocha-Chocolate Mousse

3 tablespoons sugar	1½ cups cream, whipped stiff
3 tablespoons cocoa	2 egg whites, whipped stiff
1 teaspoon instant coffee powder	

Mix the sugar with the cocoa, coffee powder, and the whipped cream. Then fold in the stiffly beaten egg whites. Chill. Serve as is, or the mousse may be used to fill Krumkaker.

Leg of Lamb, Parsleyed

1 leg of lamb	½ cup sour cream
1 cup finely chopped parsley	salt and pepper to taste

Cut about a dozen little slits or pockets in the lamb with a small sharp knife. The cuts should penetrate well into the meat. Stuff the slits or pockets tightly with chopped parsley; salt and pepper the meat all over the outside, and place in a roasting pan. Roast in a preheated 350° oven for about two hours — a little less if you like it pink, as the French do. Remove the roast when done, to "draw" in a warm place for a few minutes while you make the gravy by pouring half a cup of boiling water onto the pan drippings, then stirring in the sour cream and adding a little salt and pepper.

When you carve the leg of lamb, you should find a little circle or two of parsley in each slice.

Boneless Birds (Benløse Fugler)

1½ pounds coarsely ground
    beef

2 boiled potatoes, mashed

¾ cup milk

1 egg

1 teaspoon salt

½ pound very finely ground beef
    (grind, or have butcher grind,
    5 or 6 times)

marrow from several beef bones
    (about ⅔ cup raw marrow)

1 tablespoon dried parsley

1 teaspoon ground ginger

12 whole cloves, coarsely ground
    or crushed

1 teaspoon coarse black pepper

1 cup beef stock or consommé

2 tablespoons sour cream

Work together the coarsely ground beef with the potatoes, milk, egg, and the salt.

On a floured board make a fairly large (size of a saucer) flat meat cake from this mixture. Place a walnut-size lump of the finely ground meat in the center of the meat cake. In a separate small bowl mix together the coarsely chopped marrow, dried parsley, ginger, cloves, and pepper. Place one teaspoon of this mixture in the center of your lump of finely-ground beef, covering it completely, then fold up the coarser meat mixture all around this, forming the whole into a slightly oblong meatball. Continue as above, counting one meatball per person, as they will be fairly large. Roll them in flour, and then lightly in bread crumbs. Sauté in butter, browning well all

over. Add stock or consommé to pan, let simmer twenty
minutes in this with a lid on, turning the meatballs from time
to time. When done, add sour cream, stirring in little by little
and heating well. Serve with chopped parsley sprinkled on
top.

Marinated Beef (Surstek)

This is a delicious, succulent dish, that may be made with one
of the less expensive cuts of beef. You have to think of it almost
a week before you are going to eat it, although once put to
marinate, it needs almost no attention. A piece of chuck or
bottom round, anything you might use for pot roast, is suitable.

4 to 5-pound piece of beef	2 tablespoons butter
½ pound pork fat	1 cup stock or consommé
2 quarts buttermilk	⅔ cup sour cream (or save some
salt and pepper to taste	of the buttermilk)

Lard the meat with eight or ten thin strips of pork, using a
larding needle if you have one, or piercing the meat with a
long thin knife. Put the meat in a bowl, and pour buttermilk
over, to cover. Let stand in a fairly cool place for two or three
days (the shorter time if you do not have a cool place), then
place in refrigerator for three days more, turning the meat in
the bowl once a day. (By the third day I don't care for the looks
of the buttermilk, so I usually pour most of it off and pour
fresh buttermilk on. This is done purely from an aesthetic
sense, and its place in this recipe is quite arbitrary.) When
marinated the proper length of time, remove the meat from the
buttermilk and wipe it dry. Salt and pepper the surface of the
meat, melt butter in a deep iron pot, or Dutch oven, put the

meat in, and brown well on all sides. Add the stock and simmer with the lid on in a 350° oven for two to three hours, until the meat is tender when pierced with a fork. Add more stock if necessary during cooking. When roast is done, remove from pot and place on a serving platter. Add two-thirds cup sour cream (or buttermilk) to juices in pot, and serve as gravy with the meat.

This dish definitely calls for mashed or boiled potatoes. It is very good the next day, sliced and reheated in the gravy.

Snow Peas (Sukkererter)

These peas, eaten pod and all, are a favorite dish in such disparate cooking as French, Norwegian, and Chinese.

Snip the ends off two cups of fresh snow peas. Plunge into a pot of boiling, salted water, and boil for no more than two minutes. Drain well, add a little butter, salt and pepper, and serve. The peas should retain their fresh green color and crispness. If they are brownish and limp they have been overcooked.

Cauliflower with Shrimps (Blomkål med Reker)

1 good-sized head cauliflower	1½ cups boiled, peeled shrimps
1 teaspoon salt	dill or parsley, chopped
cream sauce	

Remove green outer leaves and soak cauliflower for twenty minutes in cold water with one teaspoon salt added. Then put cauliflower in a pot in fresh, lightly salted water, and boil until cooked but still firm, ten to twenty minutes, according to size. Drain, put on a slightly deep platter and keep warm. Make cream sauce and heat the shrimps in it for two or three minutes, then pour sauce over cauliflower, sprinkle with chopped dill or parsley, and serve.

Basic Cream Sauce

3 tablespoons butter	½ teaspoon salt
3 tablespoons flour	pinch of pepper
1½ cups whole milk or half milk, half cream	¼ teaspoon ground nutmeg

Melt butter in a saucepan over low flame, blend in flour, stirring well, and gradually add the heated milk (or milk and cream), continuing to stir until it is smooth. Add salt and pepper to taste, and nutmeg. Let boil gently for twenty minutes, continuing to stir.

Stuffed Head of Cabbage (Fyllt Kålhode)

1 medium-sized cabbage	1 chopped onion
¾ pound beef, ground	1 cup milk
¼ pound pork, ground	salt and pepper to taste
4 tablespoons cooked rice	stock

Take a firm head of cabbage, cut off a thick slice at the stem end and save. Hollow out the cabbage so that you have a cavity contained by a shell about two inches thick.

Mix together the beef, pork, rice, and chopped onion. Gradually blend in the milk, and salt and pepper. Fill the cabbage head with mixture, pressing firmly down, and close the opening with slice you cut off. Tie cabbage up firmly in a piece of cheesecloth, and boil it, preferably in stock, but may be done just in slightly salted water. Liquid should come about halfway up the cabbage, and should simmer gently with a lid on for two or three hours, depending on size of cabbage.

Remove cheesecloth, and serve stuffed cabbage with Basic Cream Sauce (see preceding page) made partly with broth cabbage has been cooked in.

Almond Rice Pudding with Fruit Sauce (Riskrem med Rød Saus)

4 tablespoons rice	almond extract (see note on
2 cups milk	page 177
⅔ cup blanched almonds, finely	1 teaspoon vanilla
chopped	½ ounce gelatin
1 tablespoon butter	¼ cup water
2 tablespoons sugar	1 cup heavy cream, whipped

Rinse the rice and scald it. Boil rice in milk till soft, add almonds, butter, sugar, almond extract, and vanilla extract. Soften gelatin in water, put softened gelatin into rice mixture while mixture is still warm, stirring and letting *cool thoroughly*. Whip cream stiff, add to rice mixture, stirring all well and mixing thoroughly. Pour into a bowl to chill in refrigerator, for at least four hours.

Fruit Sauce

> 1 cup fresh (or frozen) raspberries, or pitted cherries
> ½ tablespoon potato starch or 1 tablespoon cornstarch, stirred
> out in a little cold water

Bring the fruit to a boil, add cornstarch, let boil one minute, remove from fire. Turn Almond Rice Pudding out onto a deep serving dish or a bowl, pour the fruit sauce over, and serve. Pudding should be *very cold,* sauce warm.

Meringues

I have two basic rules for making meringues:
1) Use at least twice as much sugar as you have egg whites.
2) Bake in a very slow oven (200° to 225°).

½ cup egg whites   1¼ cups granulated sugar
pinch of salt   1 teaspoon vanilla extract

Beat the whites with the pinch of salt until they are stiff and stand in peaks. Add sugar gradually, no more than one-quarter cup at a time, and beat in. Add vanilla.

Line baking sheet with heavy wax paper, and flour this. Using a good-sized tablespoon, drop the meringues on sheet at intervals of two or three inches. Bake in very slow oven for one hour. Do not allow them to take on more than faint color. If they do, turn oven off. Test one meringue by splitting horizontally, to see if dry inside. If not, continue baking until done. Sometimes I just turn the oven off after a certain time and let them sit in it for several hours more.

Split and fill with whipped cream and berries.

For a large meringue, with chocolate-flavored whipped cream, follow mixing and whipping instructions as above, but draw a circle the size of a dinner plate on a floured cooky sheet. Place meringue mixture in circle. Being larger, this should bake about half an hour longer than the individual meringues. When cool, split meringue horizontally, and fill with one cup cream, whipped stiff, two tablespoons sugar, and three tablespoons unsweetened cocoa all mixed together.

Gooseberry Fool (Stikkelsbaergrøt)

Take a quart of gooseberries, red, yellow, or green, and remove the little stems and the blossom end. The berries do not
need to be entirely ripe. Put them in a pot with water not
quite covering them, and cook until they are soft. Add sugar
to taste, depending on the tartness of the berries. Add one
tablespoon potato starch, stirred out in a little cold water, to
each two cups of cooked berries. Let come to a boil, stir well
once, and remove from the fire. Cool, and serve with plain
cream.

Red Berry Fool (Rødgrøt)

This is made in about the same way, with the juice of any red
berries you have boiled and strained. Add sugar to taste, and in
this case, since you do not have the bulk of the fruit to thicken,
add one tablespoon potato starch, stirred out in a little cold
water, to each cup of fruit juice. After adding potato starch,
let boil one minute, then remove from the fire immediately,
or it will become rubbery. Pour the Rødgrøt into the bowl
in which it will be served, sprinkle a little sugar on top while
still hot, cool, and serve with plain cream. For texture, a crisp
cooky goes well with this.

Egg Foam (Eggedosis)

6 egg yolks	Madeira or brandy to taste
6 tablespoons sugar	(for adults only!)
2 egg whites	

Sit down in a comfortable chair, with a bowl in your lap, into which you have put the egg yolks and the sugar. Take a spoon and begin stirring. Stir and stir, daydreaming, but not stopping your stirring. Before you know it, the sugar will have been absorbed into the yolks, and you will have a lovely, smooth, pale yellow cream in your bowl. Whip the two whites separately and fold in. (Add brandy or Madeira according to your own individual needs.) Use as a dessert sauce for berries or pieces of leftover cake. It is very good poured over canned peaches.

If you are really in a hurry, use a wire whisk to beat your yolks and sugar. And if you don't taste, as you whip along, the child that you were has completely vanished!

Lamb and Cabbage Stew (Fårikål)

2 tablespoons butter	1 tablespoon whole white
4 pounds shoulder lamb chops,	peppercorns
cut into 1½-inch-square	1 tablespoon flour
pieces	potatoes, to boil
1 large head of cabbage	salt to taste
1½ cups stock (just water may	
be used instead)	

Melt one tablespoon butter in a heavy pot, and brown the pieces of lamb slightly on all sides. Add half the head of cabbage, cut into pieces, the stock (or water), and the whole peppercorns. Put a tight lid on your pot, see that the stew is simmering, and let it cook for one hour, or a little longer. Strain off the juices into a separate bowl, and put to cool, so you can skim the fat off. Reserve all the meat and the lovely disintegrated cabbage which is the mainstay of your sauce. (If there are any loose little bones, discard them.)

Put one tablespoon butter into the now empty pot to melt, add one tablespoon flour, stir, and gradually add the skimmed stock, stirring over a low flame. Put the meat back into the pot with the sauce, add the second half of the cabbage, cut into wedges, and cook for fifteen minutes more. Add salt to taste. I serve it with nice "floury" (shaken-in-the-pot) boiled potatoes.

There is an art to this. The potatoes must be boiled just enough, but not overcooked or they will fall to pieces. Having drained all water off, take the pot off the fire and, holding the lid on with one hand, move it gently back and forth and up and down until the outside of the potatoes have a dry, floury look. I suspect it is easier to do this with North European ones than with any of our Maine or Western potatoes.

Apple Cake (Eble-Kake)

4 or 5 good firm apples	½ teaspoon almond extract
1 teaspoon cinnamon	¾ cup flour
1 teaspoon powdered cardamom	1½ teaspoons baking powder
a little sugar for sprinkling	½ cup milk
2 eggs	½ cup slivered almonds
⅓ cup sugar	whipped cream
2 tablespoons butter	

Note. There is now on the market a thick white almond extract, of very good but far stronger flavor than the clear kind. A few drops of this new extract is sufficient.

Peel and core the apples, and cut into thin slices. Place in the bottom of a baking dish, and sprinkle with the cinnamon, cardamom, a little sugar. Beat the eggs, one-third cup sugar, and the softened butter together until smooth, adding the al-

mond extract. Sift flour with baking powder and add alternately with the milk, stirring well. Put this batter over the
apple slices, and bake in a 350° oven for about fifty minutes.
When about half baked, sprinkle the top with the slivered
almonds. Top with whipped cream, and serve directly from
the baking dish.

Poached Sea Trout or Salmon (Avkokt Laks)

If you are going to cook an entire fish as large as a salmon, or
even a good sized sea trout, an oblong fish-cooker is indispen-
sable. The cooker sits across two burners, giving even heat the
length of the fish. The rack is also helpful in lifting the cooked
fish from the pot and draining it. There are several ways of
poaching fish — some people like to use a court bouillon —
but since our fish in Norway was always of the freshest, Karen
poached it quite simply, relying on the good quality and flavor
of the fish itself.

Place the whole fish in the fish-cooker, having removed the
head and tail if there is not enough room. Put in enough cold
water to slightly more than cover the fish. Add a few sprigs
of parsley, a few whole white peppers, and a handful of fresh
dill, if you have it. Bring to a boil over high heat, then immediately turn flame down so that fish barely simmers, and
let it cook six minutes to the pound, or until it separates easily
from the backbone, when tested with a fork. Turn off the
heat under the cooker, and let the fish "rest" in the water five
to ten minutes longer. This makes it firmer and keeps it from
being dry. If the fish is going to be served cold, let it cool
entirely in the water it was poached in.

To serve hot, lift from the cooker, letting all the water drain off well, then slide off gently onto a large oval platter. Pour melted butter with chopped parsley over the fish, and serve it with boiled potatoes and thinly sliced cucumber salad.

Herring Pancakes (Sildepannekaker)

salt and pepper to taste
½ cup flour
24 small fresh herring 4 to 6 inches long, split and cleaned, head and tails removed

clarified butter for browning (see page 166)
3 eggs
½ cup milk
1 tablespoon chopped chives

Mix salt and pepper with the flour. Roll the fish in this. Put butter in a pan, and brown slightly without burning. Place six little fish in the pan, their tail ends meeting in the middle, the fish placed like the spokes of a wheel. Brown the fish, turning carefully one with a spatula.

Beat the eggs and milk together and add the chopped chives. Pour enough of this mixture over the fish to make a thin pancake, using six small fish for each pancake. Fry to a light brown, and then remove to a platter, folding pancakes over in half. A little brown butter may be poured over.

My Fish and Vegetable Chowder (Min Fiskesuppe)

3 pounds fresh cod or haddock
12 whole white peppers
1 tablespoon parsley, chopped
1 bay leaf, dill to taste
3 or 4 carrots, in 1-inch pieces
2 or 3 small white onions, cut in half

1 small head cauliflower, separated into flowerets
2½ cups milk
1 cup thin cream
a tiny pinch of Nepal pepper
salt to taste
chopped dill

Set whole piece or pieces of fish over fire, in enough cold water to cover. Add the whole peppers, parsley, bay leaf, and dill, and let simmer until fish comes away from the bone easily. Take fish out of pot, remove all skin and bones, and flake it into fairly large pieces. Boil down fish stock until it is reduced by half. In the meantime, in another pot place the cut-up carrots, the onions, and the cauliflower, all together, and cover with one and one-half cups water. When cooked (but not too soft) add these vegetables, and the water they were cooked in, to the reduced fish stock. Add heated milk and cream to this, and a small pinch of Nepal pepper. Salt according to taste.

Put fish back into pot with all the other ingredients and heat well. Serve in a large soup tureen, or individual large soup bowls, with chopped dill sprinkled on top for garnish. A good dish for Sunday night supper, accompanied by a loaf of French bread.

Fish au Gratin (Fiske Kreteng)

1½ cups leftover boiled fish	salt and pepper to taste
(halibut, cod, or haddock)	bread crumbs (to sprinkle on top)
2 small boiled potatoes	2 tablespoons butter
¾ cup medium cream	chopped parsley
2 eggs, separated	

Flake the fish and dice the potatoes, quite small. Add fish and potatoes to the cream. Add the two egg yolks, slightly beaten, and salt and pepper. Whip the two egg whites stiff, and fold into the mixture, blending well. Put mixture into a buttered baking dish, sprinkle a few bread crumbs on top, and bake in 400° oven for twenty to twenty-five minutes, or until a fork stuck into the middle comes out dry. Pour the melted butter and chopped parsley over it, and serve from baking dish.

Finnebu Recipes

Lingonberries with Rice (Tyttebaer med Ris)

½ cup rice   vanilla bean
2 cups milk   preserved lingonberries
2 tablespoons sugar

This is a simple dessert, made from preserves of the little red highland cranberries (lingonberries), smaller and tarter than our large American ones.

Boil the rice in milk until soft. Add the sugar and stir. Put the rice into a bowl to cool, stick a vanilla bean into it, and let cool thoroughly so that the flavor of the vanilla bean penetrates the rice well. Mix the rice with an equal amount of preserved lingonberries, and serve with plain cream.

Sugared Currants (Rørte Rips)

Pull the ripe berries off their stems with the tines of a fork. Put the berries in a bowl, being sure there are no twigs or leaves left on, and between each half cupful of berries, sprinkle a good layer of sugar. Put a vanilla bean into the bowl, and let stand overnight. Remove the vanilla bean before serving; it will have left its lovely flavor in the bowl of berries.

Waffles, Norwegian Style

There are several recipes for waffles, but I like this one which is not too rich. They can be made in any modern waffle iron, but I make mine in a small black iron Scandinavian one, which turns out a much thinner, crisp heart-shaped waffle. (The only trouble is that they are so crisply dainty that you eat too many of them!)

1 scant cup flour	1 teaspoon sugar
1 teaspoon baking powder	1 egg white, beaten stiff
¼ cup butter	1 cup sweet milk
1 egg yolk	¼ cup sour milk (or buttermilk)

Sift flour and baking powder together. Cut in the softened butter as for pastry. Combine egg yolk and sugar, then add milk and sour milk (or buttermilk), beating all together. Fold in beaten egg white. Bake in preheated, greased, waffle iron.

Wild Strawberry Jam

It takes a keen eye and infinite patience to find and pick enough wild strawberries to make jam, but it is well worth the trouble.

1 cup wild strawberries, hulled and washed	¾ cup sugar
	½ cup water

Put berries and water in a small saucepan, and let come to a boil. Add sugar and continue to boil for five minutes more. *Gently.* Remove the berries with a slotted spoon, and continue to boil just the syrup, quite rapidly, for five to ten minutes more, until it thickens slightly. Pour the syrup over the berries, and transfer the jam to small glass jars. Serve to your nearest and dearest.

Veal Patties (Kalvekarbonadekaker)

2 eggs	1 tablespoon freshly ground
1¼ cups medium cream (or milk)	pepper
8 zwieback	1 tablespoon nutmeg
2 tablespoons parsley, chopped	1 pound veal, ground together
fine	twice with
½ tablespoon salt	¼ pound fresh pork

Beat eggs slightly and mix in the cream or milk. Crush or grind zwieback fine. (I put them, a few at a time, in a clean kitchen towel, or wax paper, on a board, and crush them with a rolling pin, or they may be ground in a blender.) Add zwieback crumbs to the cream and egg. Add the parsley, salt, pepper, and nutmeg, blending all well. Gradually incorporate all this into your meat, mixing well together.

Form into small flat cakes, like a hamburger, but no more than two inches across. Cook in butter over fairly slow heat for about ten minutes, turning once, as veal and pork must always be thoroughly cooked. Remove the meat patties from the pan, and swirl a little water and a few spoonfuls of cream around in the pan and pour over.

These veal patties are very good reheated, and also freeze very well. They seem to have an affinity for cauliflower, which I serve, plain boiled, with them.

Squab Chickens, Pot Roasted

small chickens	1 cup chicken stock
salt and pepper	½ cup sour cream
butter	½ cup sweet cream

Get the smallest, plumpest little chickens you can find. Cornish game hens, weighing just about a pound, are the nearest comparable thing to the tender little chickens we used to cook in Årdal.

Wash and dry them well, salt and pepper the insides, put a big lump of butter (size of a walnut) in an iron pot, on top of the stove, and put the trussed chickens in whole, browning them well on all sides. Add a scant cup of chicken stock, put the lid on the pot, and simmer over a low flame for about forty-five minutes or until tender when pierced by a fork. Remove the chickens to a platter, discard the string, and keep them warm. Reduce the stock in the pot by half, add half a cup of sour cream and half a cup of sweet cream, and let come to a boil. Serve with the birds, separately. Cranberry or currant jelly goes well with this.

Bacon Pancakes (Fleske Pannekaker)

½ cup flour	2 eggs
1 cup milk	12 slices bacon, cut a little thick
2 tablespoons melted butter	1 teaspoon finely chopped parsley

Mix together the flour, milk, melted butter, and eggs, beating until you have a smooth batter. Set aside. Cut the bacon into squares, and fry them, then put on paper to drain. Heat a small frying pan and melt enough clarified butter in it to coat the pan well. Put a quarter of the cooked bacon into the pan, pour enough batter over to cover, sprinkle a little chopped parsley on, and cook until the bottom side is light brown, and the top side is dry. Turn to brown other side for a few seconds, then slip off onto a plate, folding in half as you do. Continue, using rest of bacon and batter.

This is a good quick luncheon or supper dish, served with a salad, and one that children usually like.

Smoked Fish, Årdal Style

2 pounds smoked fish (haddock or cod)	1 cup thin cream sauce
	a little chopped parsley
3 potatoes, boiled	2 hard-boiled eggs
1 tablespoon butter	

Remove all bones from fish, and cut into bite-size pieces. Dice the boiled potatoes, and place fish and potatoes in a shallow buttered baking dish. Cover this with a thin cream sauce. (See recipe on page 172.) To make a thin cream sauce, use more milk than basic recipe calls for, and if you are being calorie-conscious, use plain milk to bake fish and potatoes in, instead of cream sauce. Bake in a moderate (350°) oven for twenty minutes. Garnish with a little chopped parsley and quarters of hard-boiled eggs.

Brook Trout ("Vassaura")

My own little trout, known as "Vassaura" in the Årdal dialect.

Catch a nice little brook trout, about six to eight inches long. Get someone else to split and clean it. Fill it full as possible of chopped parsley, held together with a bit of butter. Tie the fish together with thread, dust lightly with flour, sauté in butter in a small pan, cut off the strings, discard them, and immediately eat the crisp brown fish with the tender white flesh.

Bonnyclabber (Rømmekolle)

Pour slightly sour raw milk into individual bowls, allowing a pint per bowl. Let stand undisturbed for a day or two until the milk is set. The top will be a thick layer of cream, the milk underneath will have the consistency of junket. Serve in individual bowls and sprinkle with sugar and zwieback crumbs.

Veal Paprikash, Norwegian Style

A polyglot dish!

   2 medium-size yellow onions, sliced
   1 tablespoon butter
1½ pounds veal, cut into small, thin pieces (scaloppine, if your butcher is Italian)
   1 heaping teaspoon paprika. (I use real Hungarian paprika, sweet and hot mixed half and half.)
   1 cup stock, made from veal scraps and bones, or chicken soup from a can, if you are not a stock-maker
   1 teaspoon flour
   ½ cup sour cream
salt to taste

Cook the onions in a little butter until they are soft and clear. Remove from pan and put to one side. Dust the pieces of veal lightly with flour, add a little more butter to pan, and sauté the meat on both sides. Add paprika, return the onions to the pan, and pour stock over the meat and onions. Put a lid on and simmer over low flame for half an hour, or until meat is tender when pierced with a fork. Stir one teaspoon flour into the sour cream, add this gradually to pan, stirring in to blend with the stock. (If stock has boiled away and sauce is too thick, add a little more stock.) Season to taste with salt, and serve. May be made ahead of time, put into a casserole and re-heated. Noodles are good as an accompaniment.

Scrambled Eggs with Smoked Salmon (Røkelaks med Eggerøre)

6 eggs
6 tablespoons cream or milk
2 tablespoons finely chopped chives

salt and pepper to taste
2 tablespoons butter
4 slices smoked salmon

Beat eggs and cream, or milk, in a bowl until just mixed. Add chives, salt, and pepper. Melt butter in a pan and cook egg mixture over low heat, using a wooden spoon to scrape mixture from bottom of pan with slow strokes, until soft lumps form. Serve immediately with a slice of smoked salmon on the side for each portion.

Thinly sliced pumpernickel spread with sweet butter is good with this. Tasty for Sunday morning breakfast, or as a light supper dish.

Marinated Salmon (Gravlaks)

A middle cut of a nice spring salmon is best for this.

Marinade
For each pound of salmon:

2 tablespoons salt	1 teaspoon white peppercorns,
2 tablespoons sugar	coarsely ground
pinch of saltpeter	plenty of dill
spruce twigs	

Slit the salmon along the backbone. Remove the backbone and all other small bones remaining. Mix the salt, sugar, and saltpeter, and rub mixture nto the salmon. Put a layer of small spruce twigs in the bottom of a shallow dish. On this put half of the salmon, skin side down. Sprinkle with pepper and lots of dill. Put the other half of salmon on top with skin side up. Cover well with dill. Put a weighted chopping board on top of the salmon, and leave in a cool dark place for forty-eight hours. It is now ready to serve.

Cut into small slanting strips. Remove the skin, and any twigs or dill clinging to it. Serve with thin-sliced buttered pumpernickel.

Sour Cream Sauce

2 tablespoons grated horseradish, or	½ cup sour cream
3 tablespoons chopped fresh dill	¾ cup sweet cream, whipped

Mix horseradish or dill with sour cream. Fold in sweet whipped cream, blend well, and serve as accompaniment to cold fish, or smoked trout, or cold roast beef.

Sauce Verte

This is very good, served as accompaniment to any cold fish.

1 cup mayonnaise	1 tablespoon chopped dill
3 tablespoons chopped parsley	1 tablespoon chopped spinach
1 tablespoon chopped tarragon	1 teaspoon lemon juice
2 tablespoons chopped chives	

Mix all the ingredients together in a blender. The fresh spinach imparts a lovely color, but if you don't have the spinach, you can use just the herbs and add a few drops of green vegetable coloring.

Fish Cakes from Leftover Kreteng

Take one and one-half cups of leftover Kreteng (page 180), put it in a bowl, and with a fork mix a slightly beaten egg into it. Pat into small cakes, and fry in buttter until brown. Or put them under the broiler for a few minutes, turning once.

Catalani Cake (Catalani Kake)

18 lady fingers	¼ cup Spanish sherry
1 cup milk	1 cup cream, whipped
1 teaspoon vanilla	¾ cup strawberry jam

Take lady fingers and soak them in the milk, to which you have added vanilla and Spanish sherry. Line a shallow bowl with the lady fingers, and fill the center with one cup of cream, whipped, into which you have mixed three-quarters cup strawberry jam. Garnish with a strawberry on top. Chill.

Spit-in-the-Pan (Pytt-i-Panna)

2 medium-sized onions, chopped	4 boiled potatoes, diced
3 tablespoons butter	salt and pepper to taste
1½ cups cooked, diced, leftover meat (lamb, beef, veal, etc.)	eggs, 1 per person
	1 tablespoon chopped parsley

Sauté the chopped onions in a little butter until soft but not browned. Add the rest of the butter to pan, and the diced meat and potatoes, and cook over a quick fire until brown and slightly crusty. Salt and pepper to taste, and serve with a poached egg on top of the mixture for each person. Sprinkle with chopped parsley and serve.

Potato Pancake

6 cold boiled potatoes	2 eggs, slightly beaten
1 finely chopped onion	salt and pepper to taste
1 tablespoon flour	2 tablespoons butter, or frying fat

Chop the potatoes quite fine, and mix with the other ingredients, except for the butter which is put in a pan for the frying. Form a cake the size of your small pan, and fry until brown, turning once.

Very good with some cold ham and a green salad.

Yellow Pea Soup (Gul Ertesuppe), *or what-to-do-with-the-hambone-when-the-last-shred-of-meat-has-been-used*

1 hambone	1 teaspoon oregano or marjoram
2 cups dried yellow peas	1 teaspoon curry powder
2 quarts water	a little pepper
1 carrot, cut into several pieces	frankfurters (optional)
1 small onion, split in two	

Put the hambone and the dried yellow peas into a large pot, and cover with the water. Add the carrot and onion. Simmer for about two hours, stirring now and then to prevent peas sticking at the bottom. When the peas are cooked to a purée, remove the bone, and stir into the soup the oregano and the curry. Serve hot, with or without heated frankfurters, cut into one-inch pieces, a few pieces put in each individual bowl.

New Potatoes with Sour Cream

The potatoes I like best are the ones that the farmer discards as too small, or throws to his pigs. Lacking a nearby farmer, the small pink potatoes found in most markets are almost as good.

18 small *new* potatoes	1 cup sour cream
1 tablespoon butter	1 tablespoon chopped chives

Do not peel, but scrub the skins well with a stiff brush. Place in a pot of cold, salted water, bring to a boil, and cook for half an hour, or until the potatoes are easily pierced by a fork. Drain well, put a tablespoon of butter and the potatoes back in the pot, and with the lid on shake well, holding pot just slightly above the flame. Put potatoes into a serving dish, pour sour cream over, and sprinkle with chopped chives.

Beef (Bif) à la Lindstrøm

   ½ cup cream
    1 pound beef, chuck or round, no fat, ground twice
    1 teaspoon salt
pepper to taste
    4 to 6 finely diced pickled beets
    2 tablespoons finely chopped onions
    2 tablespoons finely chopped capers
    2 to 3 medium-sized potatoes, boiled and diced
    3 to 4 tablespoons butter
    1 tablespoon whole capers

Stir cream into meat vigorously, add salt and pepper. Then with a two-tined fork stir in beets, onions, capers, and potatoes. Form into cakes an inch thick and brown quickly in butter over a hot fire. Turn only once. Should be pink inside.

Remove to a hot platter, add a little hot water to butter in pan, and a tablespoon of capers (not chopped). Pour over meat and serve.

Nice with sautéed potatoes and grilled tomatoes and beer. I like the meat cakes to "sit" an hour before frying — at room temperature, even on a hot summer's day.

Blueberry Fritters

1 cup flour (scant)	2 eggs, separated
pinch of salt	¾ cup blueberries
1 teaspoon baking powder	fat for deep frying
2 tablespoons water	confectioners' sugar or Eggedosis
1 tablespoon brandy	Sauce
2 tablespoons granulated sugar	

Sift flour, salt, and baking powder together. Combine water, brandy, sugar, and egg yolks, stir, then combine with the flour, stirring until smooth. Fold in the stiffly beaten egg whites, and lastly the blueberries. Drop by spoonfuls into deep hot fat, and cook until lightly browned. Serve with a dusting of confectioners' sugar, or with Eggedosis Sauce (page 175).

Birkeli Recipes

Braised Partridge

4 partridges
salt and pepper to taste
8 strips bacon or salt pork
2 tablespoons butter
½ cup meat stock or bouillon
4 slices bread (crusts removed) sautéed in butter
4 ¼-inch slices foie gras

After partridges are cleaned, sprinkle insides with salt and pepper, and place two strips of bacon or salt pork on breast of each bird. Tie birds with string, melt one tablespoon butter in bottom of large pot, and turn birds in butter to brown on all sides. Add stock or bouillon, cover pot with lid, and let simmer on top of stove for forty-five minutes, or until birds are tender.

When birds are done, remove bacon and string, place pieces of sautéed bread on a platter, cover each piece with a slice of foie gras, and place one partridge on top of each piece of bread. Pour over a little stock from the pot. Serve lingonberry preserves with the partridges.

As a variation, the partridges are sometimes roasted with juniper berries, which grow in abundance in most northern countries. In this case, omit the foie gras on the sautéed bread.

Cloudberries (Multer)

Serve fresh, ripe cloudberries or frozen ones with a little granulated sugar and some cream. The tinned ones, which need no additional sweetening, are very good mixed with an equal amount of whipped cream. These may be purchased in most Scandinavian delicacy shops in the U.S. We also use them, mixed with whipped cream, to fill Krumkaker (page 167), or in a meringue ring.

Christmas Bread (Julebrød)

2 cups milk	½ pound seedless raisins
¾ cup sugar	½ cup finely cut citron
1 teaspoon ground cardamom	1 egg, beaten
¼ cup butter	6 cups flour (more or less)
1½ yeast cakes, dissolved in a little water	1 egg and 1 tablespoon of cream beaten together for glaze
½ teaspoon salt	

Heat milk and sugar, adding the cardamom and the butter. Cool the mixture to lukewarm, then add yeast. Add salt, raisins, citron, and beaten egg. Work well together and add enough flour to make a firm but springy dough. Cover the dough and let stand in a warm place, until doubled in bulk. Knead and form into a round loaf, which you place in a greased pie tin. Let it again rise until doubled in bulk, then bake at 350° for about one hour. Fifteen minutes before taking from oven, brush egg and cream mixture over top and sides of loaf.

Chicken-Lemon Broth

2 cups clear chicken broth
2 teaspoons lemon juice
1 whole egg, plus 1 yolk

2 tablespoons cream
pinch of salt

Heat the chicken broth and lemon juice together. Beat together the eggs and cream. Add this to the chicken broth and heat over a low flame, beating vigorously until hot and frothy. *Do not allow to boil.*

Thin Fillets of Veal, Norwegian Style (Kalvefile)

2 tablespoons butter for sautéeing
chopped parsley
2 pounds fillet of veal, cut ¼ inch
   thick

1 or 2 lemons, sliced thin (1 slice
   for each piece of meat)
salt and pepper to taste
butter balls for garnish

Make a butterball for each slice of meat, and roll it in the chopped parsley until it is completely covered. Put these butter-balls in the refrigerator until ready to serve. Slice the lemons thinly.

   Melt butter in a large pan, and when it begins to turn brown, put the pieces of veal in, and sauté them over a rather high flame until they are slightly brown on each side. Sprinkle with salt and pepper, turn the flame down, and let the meat cook through. (About five minutes.)

Place meat on a warmed platter, put a slice of lemon on each piece of meat, and on the slice of lemon place one of the parsley-rolled butterballs. Garnish each piece of meat in this way. A quick dish to make, and a good one to eat when you are tired of sauces.

Velvet Pudding (Fløielsgrøt)

3 tablespoons butter	pinch of salt
3 tablespoons flour	granulated sugar
milk	cinnamon

Melt butter, add flour gradually, stirring well over a low flame. Gradually stir into this enough hot milk to make a smooth, thick porridge.

Serve hot in a deep dish, with sugar and cinnamon sprinkled on it, and additional cold milk, or with just sugar and a little red fruit juice of some sort poured over instead of the cold milk.

The most soothing thing I know for an upset stomach — or, I am told, a hangover!

French Bread and Rolls (Franskbrød)

1 envelope granulated yeast	1 heaping tablespoon salt
⅓ cup water	5 to 6 cups flour
2 cups milk	1 egg
2 tablespoons butter	1 tablespoon cream
1 tablespoon honey	

Mix the yeast into one-third cup lukewarm water, and dissolve. Heat the milk until lukewarm, and add butter, honey, and salt. When butter is melted, add the yeast-water mix, and, gradually, the flour, stirring first, then kneading until dough is smooth and does not stick to the hands. Place it in a bowl, put a cloth over, and let rise in a warm place for two hours, or until the dough has doubled its bulk. Punch down again, and let rise for forty minutes more. Knead it again, but not too long, and divide it into long slim loaves, or into little round rolls. Let rise again until double in bulk. Cut diagonal slashes in the bread, brush both loaves and rolls with milk, and bake in 350° oven for forty minutes. Rolls will take less time than bread. Ten minutes before they are finished, brush with egg mixed with cream, which gives them a better glaze. A large pie tin full of water, set on the lower shelf of oven while baking, improves the crust.

Scotch Oatmeal Bread

This should be made with the coarsely cut Scottish or Irish oatmeal.

1 quart boiling water	2 cups oatmeal
3 tablespoons butter	1 yeast cake
2 tablespoons salt	about 9 cups white flour
½ cup molasses	

Place the hot water in a large bowl and add the butter, salt, and molasses. When butter has melted, add the oatmeal and let soak for an hour. Dissolve the yeast, and add it and the flour to oatmeal in bowl, and knead all well. It should make a firm dough. Put dough in a greased bowl and let rise until double in bulk. Knead well once more and separate into six pieces.

Grease three loaf pans, and place two pieces of dough together in each pan, having first brushed the sides where they touch each other, with oil or butter. Let raise once more, until double, and set in a 400° oven. After ten minutes reduce heat to 350° and continue baking for forty-five minutes. Makes six nice little loaves, that freeze very well.

Thin Cornbread

2 tablespoons butter	½ cup white flour (a little less)
1 tablespoon sugar	½ cup yellow cornmeal (a little
1 egg	more)
⅓ cup milk	1 teaspoon baking powder

Mix all ingredients together, stirring well. Grease well an eleven by sixteen-inch pastry pan, and spread dough thinly. Bake in moderate oven, 350°. When surface looks dry, and edges are just beginning to take on color (about fifteen minutes), remove pan and cut into squares, approximately two by three inches. Return to oven and let brown slightly until they look like melba toast.

Gnocchi, My Style

1 cup yellow cornmeal	1½ cups grated Cheddar cheese
1 cup cold water	½ cup grated Parmesan cheese
6 cups boiling water	3 egg yolks
1 cup Cream of Wheat	1 teaspoon salt
2 tablespoons butter	½ teaspoon pepper

Stir one cup cornmeal into one cup cold water. (This eliminates lumps.) Do this in the large pot you are going to cook it in. Now add six cups boiling water, and stir well. Add

gradually, beating to eliminate any lumps, one cup Cream of
Wheat. Add butter, and cook, stirring, over low flame (it
should just bubble) for about ten minutes, by which time it
should be quite heavy and hard to stir.

Add one-half cup grated Cheddar, one-half cup grated Parmesan, and the egg yolks, and stir well. Remove from stove and
pour into a buttered pan, to the depth of about an inch, and let
cool thoroughly. When cold and stiff (I usually do this part of
the Gnocchi the day before serving), cut into one-inch squares.
Butter an ovenproof dish, and pile the squares of Gnocchi
higgledy-piggledy in the dish, sprinkling with the rest of the
Cheddar, as you go. Bake in a hot oven for twenty-five minutes.
I use this recipe for large parties, as it serves fourteen to sixteen.

Country Ham Omelet

Such a good way to use up those last little scraps of ham
before the bone goes into the soup pot!

½ cup minced ham	4 or 5 eggs
1 cold boiled potato, diced fine	1 tablespoon butter
1 teaspoon minced onion or scallion tops	

Take minced ham, diced potato, and a little bit of minced
onion or scallion tops. Heat this all together in a little bit of
butter, and let it keep warm on the back of the stove.

Beat four or five eggs together with a fork, adding a tablespoon of water for each egg. Put a tablespoon of butter to melt
in your pan, and add the eggs, quickly tilting the pan and swirling around to cover all the surface. You can even scrape the
center of the pan with your spatula, to loosen the egg which has
already started to cook, and run some more of the liquid part

under it. Does this sound obscure? Try it, and you will see what I mean. Cook omelet over a fairly high flame and when brown underneath, place your ham-potato-onion mix on one half of the omelet, and fold the other half over filling. Slide off onto the waiting plate, and serve with a green salad.

Lentil Soup

2 cups lentils	1 hambone
1 quart water	1 small onion, minced
1 quart stock or bouillon	salt and pepper
1 cup red wine	

Soak two cups of lentils overnight. Next day put them in the pot with the liquid ingredients, the hambone, the onion, and seasoning. Cook until the lentils are completely soft. Remove hambone, and serve the soup.

Ham and Vegetable Stew (Skinke Lapskaus)

1 cup raw carrots, cut into small cubes	1 cup stock or bouillon
	2 teaspoons potato flour
¾ cup white turnips, cut into small cubes	1 cup ham, cut into small cubes
1 cup fresh (or frozen) peas	1 teaspoon chopped parsley

Put the cut-up carrots, turnips, and peas into a pot all together with just enough water to cover. (If you are using frozen peas, add to pot when carrots and turnips are almost done, as they need less cooking time.) Cook vegetables until just done, and save the water they were boiled in. Stir the potato flour into one-quarter cup of the cold stock or bouillon. Heat the ham in the rest of the bouillon and add ham and bouillon to the vegetables and the water they were cooked in. Add the dissolved potato flour. Stir well, let come to a boil, then turn off heat after boiling one minute. Serve with a little chopped parsley sprinkled on top.

Karen's Best Visit Cake

½ cup butter	2 teaspoons baking powder
¾ cup sugar	½ cup milk
2 eggs, separated	1 teaspoon almond extract
1½ cups flour	

Stir butter and sugar well together until blended and smooth. Add egg yolks and blend in. Sift flour with baking powder and add alternately with milk, stirring all well together. Add almond extract. Whip egg whites stiff, and fold in. Pour batter into a greased loaf pan and bake at 350° for about fifty minutes.

Of course this can be whipped up in a mixer so quickly that it is practically ready for the guests by the time they have toured the garden, admired the roses, and settled down for their tea!

Cardamom Cake

½ pound butter	grated rind of one lemon
1 cup sugar	grated rind of one orange
6 eggs	1 cup light currants, steamed until
2 cups flour	soft
2 teaspoons baking powder	1 teaspoon vanilla extract
pinch of salt	a little cinnamon and sugar mixed
1 tablespoon ground cardamom	for sprinkling top

Cream the butter and sugar together. Beat the eggs slightly and add to mixture, stirring all well together. Save a little of the flour to flour the currants. Sift the rest of the flour together with the baking powder, salt, and the cardamom. Add the grated rinds, the floured currants, and the vanilla. Stir well. Grease a loaf pan well, and spread your mixture evenly in it. Sprinkle top generously with cinnamon and sugar. Bake at 350° for about one hour.

Golden Sponge Cake

6 eggs, separated	2 teaspoons grated lemon rind
1 cup sugar	1¼ cups cake flour
¼ cup cold water	½ teaspoon baking powder
2 teaspoons lemon juice	pinch of salt

Beat egg yolks and sugar together until very thick and yellow. Beat in the cold water, the lemon juice, and the lemon rind. Add the cake flour, sifted with the baking powder. Whip egg whites stiff, with a pinch of salt, and fold into mixture. Pour batter into an ungreased nine-inch tube pan, and bake in a 325° oven for one hour. Invert pan immediately, but let cake cool in it before you remove it from the pan. This cake should never be cut with a knife, but pulled apart with a fork.

Linser Cakes

When I was a child I always called these little puffy heart-shaped cookies "lommer" (pockets). I suppose this was because I knew there was something nice inside them that was hidden. It was traditional to make these cakes with a custard filling. Grandmother found this too bland, so Karen filled them instead with Lemon Curd.

1¼ cups flour	1 egg yolk
3 tablespoons sugar	7 tablespoons butter

Mix these ingredients together on a pastry board or right on the table. Work them together until the pastry is smooth, then set in a cool place to chill.

Lemon Curd Filling

3 eggs, separated	1 cup sugar
½ cup butter	½ cup lemon juice

Beat eggs until light. Melt butter in a double boiler, over hot but not boiling water. Add to the butter 1 cup granulated sugar, and the eggs, stirring well. Cook over hot water stirring constantly until it begins to thicken. Add one-half cup lemon juice, and cook a few minutes longer until thick and smooth. Chill.

Roll out two thirds of the pastry. Line small greased, shallow, heart-shaped tins with the dough. Put the cooled lemon filling into the lined tins. Roll out the remaining dough and make lids over the filling, pinching the edges well together. Bake fifteen to twenty minutes in a 400° oven.

Fresh Pea Soup (Blender Made)

In those pre-electric blender days, Karen made all her vegetable soups by puréeing them through a fine sieve. Now, with our wonderful modern blenders, good soups can be made quickly and economically, out of a few vegetables that might otherwise go to waste.

1 cup fresh or frozen green peas	½ teaspoon curry powder
2 cups chicken broth	½ teaspoon dried thyme
½ cup milk (cream is even better!)	salt and pepper

Boil fresh or frozen peas for five minutes. Place in blender with broth, add milk, curry, thyme, salt and pepper. Blend until quite smooth, then reheat.

I serve this with fried croutons of bread, rolled in a little curry powder. A few croutons dropped into each soup bowl.

Chanterelle Mushrooms (Kantareller)

One of my happiest memories from Årdal is coming through the birch woods after several days of August rains, and seeing at my feet, half-hidden by the springy green moss it grew in, the lovely orange chanterelle (*Cantharellus cibarius*), a mushroom found not only in Scandinavia, but in the northern states of our country as well.

To prepare: Wash them, dry them well, and put them in a pan with a little butter. They can be allowed to simmer in their own juices for quite a while, twenty minutes or so. Add a couple of spoonfuls of sour cream, some salt and pepper, and you have a wonderful accompaniment for a roast of lamb or veal, or for that Sunday chicken.

Almond Peach Tart (Fire Specier Fersken Kake)

½ cup sugar
½ pound plus 1 tablespoon butter
1 egg
2 cups flour

1½ cups ground blanched almonds
1 large can peach halves, preferably the white peaches

Stir sugar and butter well together, and then add the slightly beaten egg. Mix the flour into this, blending it well with the hands until all ingredients are well mixed. Add the ground almonds to the dough, again blending well.

Grease a pie or tart pan and cover with the dough, pressing it into place with the fingers, and marking around the edge of the pan with the tines of a fork. Bake the pie crust in a 350° oven for twenty minutes, then remove from the oven and cover bottom of crust with peach halves, cut side up.

Meringue topping

4 whites of eggs, beaten stiff   ½ teaspoon almond extract
¾ cup sugar

Blend these ingredients together, adding the sugar gradually to the beaten egg whites. Cover the peaches with the meringue, and put the whole thing back in the oven for twenty minutes more, or until the meringue is puffy and takes on a faint coloring.

Chinese Chicken Salad

    1 teaspoon dry mustard
    1 teaspoon lemon juice
    ½ teaspoon sesame seed oil
    4 tablespoons mayonnaise
    2 cups cooked chicken, cut into bite-sized pieces
    1 cup scallions cut slantwise into 1-inch segments (about half
        should be the green part)
    salt and pepper to taste
    peanut oil or corn oil
    bean threads (Saifun) to make 2 lightly packed cups when cooked

Blend the mustard, lemon juice, and sesame seed oil with the mayonnaise. Add this to cut-up chicken and scallions, salt and pepper, and blend well. Heat four to five inches of peanut or corn oil in a medium-sized saucepan. The oil must be hot enough so that the bean threads (which look like very thin, clear spaghetti) puff up and rise to the surface the minute they are dropped into the saucepan. (Test one or two first.) Cook only a small quantity at a time, remove from the oil, and drain on paper, as soon as they have puffed. Do not allow them to brown. Have the rest of your salad ready and mixed, and the bean threads cooked and cooled. Mix the bean threads into the salad at the last minute, blending all well together, but lightly, with two forks. Garnish the salad with a few chopped green scallions, and serve.

This salad has a particularly nice crispy-crunchy quality, especially appropriate for a warm summer day.

Norwegian Apple-Crumb Cake

4 tablespoons butter	½ teaspoon nutmeg
2 cups zwieback crumbs	2 cups sweetened apple sauce
1 teaspoon cinnamon	

Melt the butter in a pan and add the zwieback crumbs, as well as the cinnamon and the nutmeg. In an ovenproof dish place a layer of zwieback crumbs on the bottom, then a layer of apple sauce, another layer of crumbs, and another of apple sauce, then a final layer of crumbs on top. Dot with a little more butter, and bake for half an hour in a 375° oven. Serve slightly warm with Eggedosis (page 175) or custard sauce.

Custard Sauce

6 egg yolks	2 cups light cream
3 tablespoons sugar	½ cup heavy cream, whipped
3 teaspoons vanilla extract	

Beat egg yolks and sugar in top of a double boiler, heat the light cream, add to yolks, and cook until it thickens, stirring constantly. Remove from heat, add the vanilla and cool, stirring now and then. When cold, fold in the whipped cream.

Spinach Timbale

1 full cup cooked spinach, chopped fine	1 teaspoon grated nutmeg
1 teaspoon grated onion	4 whole eggs, plus 2 yolks
salt and pepper to taste	1½ cups milk

Mix the chopped spinach and the onion together. Add salt,

pepper, and nutmeg. Beat the four eggs and the two yolks into the milk. Add this to the spinach mixture.

Pour all into a well-buttered ring mold, set in a pie tin of warm water, and bake in a 350° oven for forty-five minutes, or until a knife comes out clean. Take ring mold out of oven, loosen slightly around the edge with a knife, and reverse onto a platter. Pour Mushroom Sauce over, and serve. May also be served with Tomato Sauce.

Mushroom Sauce

1 pound fresh mushrooms	1 cup bouillon (scant)
2 tablespoons butter	¾ cup sour cream
1 tablespoon flour	salt and pepper

Wash and dry mushrooms, and slice but do not peel. Melt butter in a pan, and add the mushrooms. Stir now and then and let simmer for about ten minutes. Sprinkle with flour, add bouillon and sour cream, stirring all well together. Salt and pepper to taste.

Tomato Sauce

1 medium-sized yellow onion, chopped fine	1 clove garlic, minced very fine
1 carrot, chopped fine	1 teaspoon basil
2 stalks celery, chopped fine	½ teaspoon oregano
2 tablespoons olive oil	salt and pepper to taste
1 can (1 pound 10 ounces) Italian tomatoes	

Put the chopped onion, carrot, and celery in a small pan with the olive oil, and cook until soft but not brown. Drain some of the juice from the tomatoes, and put them in a large sauce-pan. Add to them the carrots, onions, celery, garlic, basil, and oregano. Cook slowly for about an hour, or until it thickens, stirring now and then to prevent sticking at the bottom. If it seems too thick before serving, add a little of the excess tomato juice that you poured off. Salt and pepper, to taste.

Good as accompaniment to Spinach Timbale (page 211), or Délices d'Emmental, (page 240), or Stuffed Pasta Shells (page 223).

Veal Orloff, Modified

1 saddle of milk-fed veal	2 tablespoons butter
4 carrots, chopped	1 cup bouillon or meat stock
4 onions, chopped	Soubise Purée (recipe follows)
parsley, thyme	1 cup sour cream
salt and pepper	Parmesan cheese

Karen took a nice saddle of veal, tied it up securely, and put it in a roasting pan on a layer of chopped carrots and onions, with a little thyme and chopped parsley added. She salted and peppered the meat, spread two tablespoons of butter over the top of it, and put it in a preheated 350° oven for about three hours. When the meat was half roasted, she poured a cup of bouillon or meat stock over it, and basted the meat frequently with the stock and pan juices.

When cooked (veal should not be pink when done), the roast was taken from the oven, and with a very sharp knife Karen cut the saddle crosswise into three-quarter-inch-thick slices, without cutting quite through to the bottom, so that the slices remained fixed at one end, and spread the Soubise Purée between the slices, reforming the meat onto the saddle. Over this she spread the sour cream, and sprinkled it with a little grated Parmesan cheese. The roast went back in the oven for five to ten minutes more, before serving. (The pan drippings were taken off and served separately if anyone felt the need for an additional sauce!)

Soubise Purée

4 onions, minced fine	½ cup Basic Cream Sauce (see
6 tablespoons butter	page 172)
1 pound fresh mushrooms	

Mince four onions fine and place in a pan with three tablespoons of the butter. Cover pan and simmer onions gently, not letting them get brown, but cooking until they are clear and soft. Add rest of the butter and the finely chopped mushrooms. (May be done in blender.) Simmer for twenty minutes. Add cream sauce to this.

Definitely a party dish.

Blueberry-Raspberry Galette

1 cup sifted flour	1 egg yolk
½ teaspoon salt	1 tablespoon lemon juice
1 tablespoon sugar	1 tablespoon water
6 tablespoons butter	filling (next page)

Mix ingredients together and chill thoroughly. Roll or pat dough until it is about one-half inch thick and put it into an eleven-inch pie tin, or a twelve-inch galette pan (a shallow tin pan with straight fluted edges). Chill again.

Filling

2 cups blueberries	¼ cup butter, melted
¼ cup sugar	2 cups raspberries
1 teaspoon cinnamon	

Fill the unbaked, chilled galette with the fresh blueberries. Sprinkle over berries the sugar mixed with cinnamon and the melted butter. Place galette in preheated 425° oven. After twelve minutes reduce heat to 350° and bake ten minutes more, or until berries are slightly soft. Cool.

Decorate with fresh raspberries in a double circle around outer edge of galette, and a small circle in center. Serve with or without whipped cream, cutting in pie-shaped pieces.

Anchovy Sticks (Puff Pastry Hors d'Oeuvres)

The principal thing in making puff pastry is to have your ingredients chilled, to get your butter and flour properly blended, and to be able to return to the kitchen at intervals of half an hour to give the dough another turn.

This is a small portion of puff pastry, but I find it easier to handle and enough for ordinary family needs. Double for large parties.

2 cups all-purpose flour	1 cup butter
6 ounces ice water	1 tin anchovies

Put the flour in a mound on your pastry board (and don't try to make this in a very hot kitchen), make a well in the center, and pour the ice water in, little by little, mixing it with the flour with your fingertips. There should be just enough water so that it holds the flour together and you can roll it up into a firm ball. Wrap it in wax paper, and put it to chill for half an hour. Roll out this dough until you have an oblong about half an inch thick. Flatten your butter and shape it into a square that you can place in the center of the dough, folding up the four sides over it, to envelop it completely. Give it a small flattening, to hold all the edges closed over the butter, wrap it in wax paper, and put it to chill in refrigerator for half an hour. (If you get involved doing something elsewhere it doesn't matter: it's good for the dough to "rest.")

Roll it out again into an oblong, trying not to let the butter break through. Place it with the long side facing you, and fold left end over, then corresponding right end, so that you again have an approximate square. Do this four times in all, letting dough rest half an hour in between each turn. The butter should be thoroughly incorporated by now, but if not, give it one more turn.

Now roll out an oblong of your pastry no more than one-eighth inch thick. Drain a tin of straight, not rolled, anchovies. Place anchovies about two inches apart on the pastry, cut pastry off evenly between each one, and fold pastry over anchovy, sticking together at edges by moistening slightly. (I simply dip my finger into a glass of water, and wet the edges that way.) Rinse off a baking sheet with cold water, place anchovy sticks on this about two inches apart, brush tops of pastries with a little beaten egg, and let chill again for fifteen minutes.

Place in a preheated 450° oven. After ten minutes turn oven down to 350°, and let bake until puffed and light brown. You will have some pastry left over to make other things.

Cheese Turnovers (Ostelapper)

An hors d'oeuvre similar to Anchovy Sticks was made with a small square of cheese substituting for the anchovy. Follow directions in preceding recipe, making pastry square in shape instead of long. Any fairly hard cheese can be used — Swiss, "rat-trap" (Cheddar), etc.

This same puff pastry lends itself to dessert pastries, such as napoleons, as you will see on page 229.

Chicken Suzanne

2 pounds small white onions	1 cup chicken broth
½ pound butter	1 tablespoon flour (scant)
2 small broilers, each cut into quarters	1 cup heavy cream
	4 ounces port or Dubonnet

Cook the onions in half the butter in a double-boiler, for one hour. Melt the rest of the butter in a large pan, and brown the pieces of chicken in it, turning well on all sides. When brown, pour off the butter from the chicken, pour the chicken broth over the pieces in the pan, put a lid on and let simmer for about thirty minutes, or until tender.

When chicken is cooked, take the pieces and put them into a casserole, keeping it warm. Reduce the stock in pot by one third. Stir the flour into the cream, add this to reduced stock, add port wine or Dubonnet, stir, and bring to a boil. Add to this the onions, with a little of the butter they were cooked in. (Save the rest of the butter for your next onion-flavored dish.) Pour this sauce with onions over chicken in casserole, and serve with rice.

Caramel Pudding (Crème Caramel)

1¼ cups sugar	2 cups milk
¾ cup boiling water	pinch of salt
4 eggs plus 2 yolks	1 teaspoon vanilla extract

Put sugar in an iron pan over slow heat, and stir with a wooden spoon until it turns an even, caramel-colored yellow. Slowly pour into it three-quarters cup boiling water, and continue to stir until sugar and water are blended. Pour this syrup into a deep baking dish, and swirl it around to coat the inside.

Beat the eggs and milk together and add salt and vanilla extract. Pour into the caramel-coated dish, set dish in a pan containing at least an inch of hot water, place in a slow (325°) oven, and bake until custard is set. (Test by sticking a pointed knife into center. It is done when knife comes out clean.)

Must cool thoroughly and "set" awhile. Is best when made in the morning to be eaten that night, or even the next day.

Birthday Breakfast Cake (Fødselsdagskringle)

3 eggs	1 tablespoon ground cardamom
¾ cup milk (scant)	½ cup candied orange or lemon
4 cups flour	peel, cut up fine
2 cakes yeast	coarse sugar
2 tablespoons sugar	1 cup blanched, slivered almonds
½ pound butter (scant)	

Beat the eggs, mix into the milk, and add the sifted flour. Dissolve yeast in a little lukewarm water and add to it the sugar and the melted butter, the cardamom, and the chopped peel. Add this to the dough and knead well. The dough should be quite firm. Allow the dough to rise in a warm place for half an hour, then knead again. Wrap the dough up in a cloth, wrung out in cold water, and place in the refrigerator overnight. (Karen placed it in the coolest part of the cellar.) Take out of refrigerator early in the morning, let rise for half an hour, divide in two, and roll out in the shape of two long sausages. Place the two pieces on a greased baking sheet, to form the traditional figure 8 with one straight side (like the gilded signs hanging outside the bakers' shops in all of Scandinavia).

Let rise twenty minutes. Brush the top with a little slightly beaten egg, sprinkle with coarse sugar and the slivered almonds. Bake in a hot (400°) oven until nicely risen and golden brown.

No candles to light on this! But fresh flowers decorating the board or platter it is served on. A nice way to start the day, and a new year!

Bananes-en-Chemise, Dorothea

6 tablespoons butter	1 teaspoon lemon juice
½ cup firmly packed dark brown sugar	4 bananas, split lengthwise
	8 basic crêpes (page 165)
pinch of salt	½ cup rum or cognac

Melt the butter and add the brown sugar, a pinch of salt, and the lemon juice. Put the banana halves, side by side, in a baking dish and pour the sugar mixture over. Bake twenty minutes in a 400° oven. Take the bananas carefully out of the baking dish, saving all the lovely sugary goo. Wrap a crêpe carefully around each banana half, and replace in baking dish. Put back in the oven for five minutes more, then take out of oven, pour rum or cognac over it, and flame it!

Chicken Sebastiano

2 broilers, split	1 teaspoon chopped tarragon (fresh
½ cup olive oil	is best, dried will do)
½ cup lemon juice	1 teaspoon oregano
2 cloves garlic, minced	salt and pepper to taste

Brush some olive oil on the skin side of the chicken, and place the chicken halves, skin side down, in a shallow roasting pan. Mix together the lemon juice, olive oil, garlic, herbs, salt and pepper. Pour some of this mixture onto the chicken halves, so that about a tablespoonful is held in the hollow of each chicken half. Bake in a 350° oven for an hour, basting frequently with more of the olive oil–lemon juice mixture. After forty minutes, turn chicken halves over, and do the skin side for the last twenty minutes, so that it gets brown. If not brown enough to suit your taste, put it under the broiler for a few minutes at the end. The essential thing is to be conscientious about basting the chicken every ten or fifteen minutes.

Chicken Sauté Birkeli

2 small broilers, quartered	3 tomatoes, skinned and diced
4 tablespoons clarified butter	1½ cups heavy cream
½ teaspoon English mustard	salt and pepper to taste
1 teaspoon tomato paste	chopped parsley or tarragon

Sauté the chicken in clarified butter, turning on all sides until brown. Add the mustard, tomato paste, and diced tomatoes to chicken, and stir to mix. Pour the cream over, add salt and pepper to taste. Let simmer gently for twenty minutes to half an hour, depending on size of broilers, turning the chicken several times in the sauce.

When cooked, put pieces of chicken on a heated platter, reduce sauce if necessary by cooking a few minutes more, and pour sauce over chicken. Sprinkle with chopped parsley or a little chopped tarragon, and serve.

Sweetbreads and Ham in Sherry Sauce

2 teaspoons salt
2 tablespoons lemon juice
3 pairs sweetbreads
2 tablespoons butter
1 green pepper, seeded and chopped
2 cups cubed, cooked ham

½ pound mushrooms (tinned morels, if you can get them)
1 tablespoon flour
salt and pepper
1 cup cream
½ cup sherry

In a pot put two quarts of water, two teaspoons salt, and the lemon juice, and bring it to a boil. Add the sweetbreads, reduce the heat, and simmer covered for twenty minutes. Drain sweetbreads and plunge them into cold water. Drain, remove membrane and veins, and cut sweetbreads into bite-size pieces. Melt butter in a pan, and cook the chopped green pepper ten minutes, over medium heat, then add the ham and the cut-up sweetbreads. Add the mushrooms. (If fresh ones, slice and cook first with the green pepper.) Stir in the flour, salt, and pepper. Gradually add the heated cream and sherry, stirring, and simmer gently for five to eight minutes. Serve on toast, or with boiled rice.

Kidneys, Swiss Style

2 veal kidneys
3 tablespoons butter
1 tablespoon chopped onions and chives
¼ cup brandy (to flambé)
salt and pepper to taste

a dash of Worcestershire sauce
1 tablespoon tomato ketchup
1 tablespoon port wine
a touch of French mustard
⅓ cup heavy cream, heated

Roast the kidneys in a pan in the oven until they are partly cooked (10 minutes). Remove the fat from them, and the hard core, and slice them thin. Put butter in a pan, add the chopped onion and chives, and cook for five minutes until soft but not brown. Remove onion and chives from pan and reserve. Put the kidney slices into the same buttered pan, over a high flame, pour brandy over, and set on fire. Sauté the kidneys quickly over a high flame, then put the onions and chives back in the pan, and add the salt, pepper, Worcestershire, ketchup, port wine, and mustard. Add the heated cream. Let simmer a couple of minutes, swirling the pan to blend all ingredients well, then serve with plain boiled rice. All this must be done quickly once the kidneys are added, or they will be tough.

Ramekin Cheese Tarts

Make a dough of the following ingredients, for small tart shells.

1 cup flour   ½ cup softened butter
1 egg yolk   pinch of salt

Mix these ingredients quickly with the hands until you have a smooth dough. (Pastry should never be worked longer than necessary as this toughens it.) If necessary, a little ice water may be added to make the dough hang together so you can gather it up in a ball, wrap in wax paper, and put in refrigerator to chill for at least one hour. Roll out chilled pastry about one-eighth inch thick, and line tins with it.

Filling

½ pound Swiss Gruyère or Emmentaler cheese, grated, plus one third as much grated Cheddar or "store" cheese
1 tablespoon flour

3 eggs
1 cup light cream
1 cup milk
½ teaspoon nutmeg
salt and pepper to taste

Dredge the grated cheese with the flour, and half-fill the tart shells with this. Beat the eggs with the cream, milk, nutmeg, and salt and pepper. Pour this carefully over the cheese in the tarts, not quite filling them. Place on a cooky sheet and bake in a 400° oven for ten to fifteen minutes. When they are slightly brown and puffy, reduce heat to 350° and bake about ten minutes more, or until filling is set. Remove from tins.

Can be made ahead of time and reheated.

Stuffed Pasta Shells

Jumbo Pasta Shells (four to five to a person. Boil a few extra in case one or two of them break).

1 cup cottage cheese
1 cup chopped spinach
1 teaspoon grated onion
1 teaspoon oregano

½ teaspoon grated nutmeg
salt and pepper to taste
2 cups tomato sauce (page 212)

Boil the Jumbo Shells according to directions on package, about twelve minutes, in salted water. Drain upside down on a dry towel. Mix remainder of ingredients together, except tomato sauce, and stuff each shell with about one tablespoon of filling. Place the stuffed shells in a buttered baking dish, pour the tomato sauce over and around, and heat in 350° oven for twenty to twenty-five minutes. Serve with a green salad.

Kolkauna

2 large onions	pinch of salt and pepper
¾ cup bouillon	1 pound pork sausages or Mid-
6 medium-sized potatoes	dagspølse (veal and beef sau-
3 tablespoons butter	sage)
⅓ cup hot milk	

Cut onions into slices and boil in bouillon until soft. Boil the potatoes, drain, and mash them, adding the butter, milk, salt and pepper. When thoroughly mashed, add the boiled onions and one-third cup of the bouillon they were boiled in. Mix well together, and arrange the potato-onion mix in a mound on a platter. Put the cooked sausages nicely around the mound of potatoes, and pour over a little of the drippings from the pan. Serve with a mixed green salad.

Praline Whip (Krokankrem)

1 cup sugar	1 egg yolk
¾ cup blanched almonds	1¼ cups heavy cream
¼ teaspoon cream of tartar	1 tablespoon sugar
¼ cup water	

Combine one cup sugar, almonds, cream of tartar, and water in a saucepan, and cook without stirring until the mixture is the color of dark molasses. Pour out immediately onto an oiled or buttered cooky sheet, and allow to cool and harden. When cool, crush it, which can be done in a number of ways. An easy way, if you have a blender, is to put small quantities at a time into the blender and grind it up. I prefer to put the brittle into a wooden bowl and pound and break it up with a wooden mallet or potato masher. It takes a little more work, but the pieces of almond brittle that are the basis of your dessert are slightly assorted in size, rather than all pulverized equally. However, this is a matter of time and taste. Stir the egg yolk with one tablespoon sugar, until smooth and creamy. The ground almond brittle is mixed well with the stiffly whipped cream and the egg, and the whole beautiful toothsome mass put into a bowl to chill, or in the freezer, if you prefer it slightly frozen. Any way you make it you will linger happily over each spoonful you put into your mouth.

Veal Chops en Casserole

6 veal chops, about an inch thick	salt and pepper
2 tablespoons brandy	½ cup veal stock or bouillon
2 carrots, chopped	1 tablespoon sherry
1 small white turnip, chopped	1 teaspoon flour
1 dozen small white onions	½ cup cream
½ teaspoon tarragon	

Brown the veal chops in butter in a skillet. Pour the heated brandy over them, and set fire. Place chops in a casserole on a layer of chopped carrots and turnip. Brown the whole onions for five minutes in the skillet with a little more butter, then add to the casserole. Add tarragon, salt and pepper, and stock. Place casserole in the oven, with a lid on, and cook until tender, about an hour. Add sherry, and flour stirred out in the cream. Let cook a few minutes more to blend tastes well, and serve.

Swiss Potatoes

6 good-sized potatoes	1 cup grated Emmentaler or
1 teaspoon salt	Gruyère cheese
½ teaspoon pepper	3 tablespoons butter

Peel the potatoes, slice thin (if they are "wet," pat them dry with a towel). Place a layer in the bottom of a small, deep, buttered baking dish. Sprinkle with salt and pepper, grated cheese, and with small dots of butter all over. (This dish depends on just how you dot the butter, so the potatoes cook evenly in it.)

Continue the layers of potatoes, cheese, and butter until dish is filled. Last layer on top should be cheese and butter. Bake in a 350° oven for about one hour, or until the potatoes are cooked, and crisp and brown on top.

Strawberry Soufflé

1 quart fresh strawberries (or 2 packages frozen)	¼ cup Curaçao or orange liqueur
	6 egg whites
½ cup granulated sugar	½ cup confectioners' sugar

Wash one quart of fresh ripe strawberries and hull them. (Or use 2 boxes frozen strawberries, thawed.) Put the berries through a strainer, reserving a little excess juice. Put one-half cup granulated sugar, and one-quarter cup Curaçao, or orange liqueur, into the strawberry purée, and mix well. Beat six egg whites very stiff, gradually adding half a cup of confectioners' sugar. Fold whites gently into the strawberry mix. Butter a soufflé dish, sprinkle it with granulated sugar, and pour soufflé mixture into it. Bake at 350° for twenty to twenty-five minutes, until puffed up and pale brown.

Sauce

Add to the excess juice one-quarter cup Curaçao and a little potato starch or cornstarch to thicken it. Bring to a quick boil, take off the fire, and serve with the soufflé. Keep a few whole strawberries aside, to put into the sauce.

Risi-Bisi

3 tablespoons butter	3¾ cups chicken stock
1 medium-sized onion, chopped fine	½ cup finely cut ham, or
2 small sticks of celery, chopped fine	4 slices bacon, fried crisp and crumbled
1 cup rice	3 tablespoons Parmesan cheese
1 cup shelled peas, frozen or fresh	salt and pepper to taste
	parsley, chopped

Melt half the butter in a saucepan and cook the chopped onion and celery over low heat until soft but not brown. Add rice to pan and stir until translucent. In the meantime, cook the peas separately until done. Pour the heated stock over the rice, bring to a boil, then turn heat low to simmer, and put a lid on the saucepan. Simmer about twenty minutes, or until the rice is soft. The rice should be moist and the stock almost absorbed. Add the peas, chopped ham or bacon, remaining butter, grated Parmesan cheese, salt and pepper. Mix all well together, and serve with a little chopped parsley on top.

Blueberry Fool (Blabaergrøt)

| 1 cup sugar | 2 tablespoons potato flour |
| 3 cups blueberries | ½ cup cold water |

Wash blueberries and remove any little stems or leaves. Put in a pot to cook with one cup of granulated sugar for each three cups of berries. Stir potato flour into cold water, and when the berries have boiled for five minutes, add this to the pot. Stir, boil for one minute more, and remove from the fire. Pour into the bowl in which it is to be served, sprinkle a little powdered sugar on top, and cool. Serve with cream.

Blueberry Tarts

1 recipe galette pastry (see page 214)	1 teaspoon lemon juice
2 cups blueberries	½ teaspoon cinnamon
¾ cup sugar	½ cup currant jelly

Fill small well-greased tart tins with a thin layer of galette or flan pastry. Mix two cups washed fresh blueberries with three-quarters cup sugar, one teaspoon lemon juice, and one-half teaspoon cinnamon. Fill tart shells with this mixture and bake in a 350° oven until pastry is light brown. Remove from oven, cool, and glaze with a little currant jelly, heated and thinned with a few drops of water.

Cream Puffs (Pâte à Choux)

This recipe for Pâte à Choux is the one I prefer, as the slight preponderance of water over flour makes it lighter and less tough than the usual recipe. If you find the insides of your

puffs a little too soft, remove some of the inside when you split
them, before filling.

½ cup butter	1 tablespoon sugar
1½ cups hot water	1¼ cups flour
pinch of salt	4 eggs (not too large)

Put the butter in a saucepan and pour the hot water over it.
When the butter is melted, add salt and sugar and bring to a
boil. Add all the flour at once and stir vigorously until the
mixture forms a kind of ball, and leaves the sides of the pot.
Take the pot off the flame, and add the eggs, one by one, stirring well until they are mixed into the dough and the mixture
is thick and glossy. (I use both a wooden spoon and a small
wire whisk, alternately, for this.) Drop batter onto a buttered
baking sheet, from a teaspoon (for small "mouthful" puffs) or
from a tablespoon (for dessert-size puffs).

Bake in a hot (425°) oven for ten minutes, then reduce heat
to 350° and bake until puffs are brown and crisp with no beads
of moisture on them. Cool on wire rack, split, and fill with
flavored whipped cream. This amount makes one large ring,
or six to eight large puffs or about sixteen small ones.

A cup of cream, whipped, and mixed with one cup of raspberry jelly, makes a good filling.

Napoleons

puff pastry (see page 215)	1½ teaspoons cornstarch
1 cup cream	4 tablespoons red currant jelly
2 egg yolks	½ cup confectioners' sugar
1 tablespoon sugar	1 tablespoon water
1 teaspoon vanilla	

Divide the dough into two parts and roll out thin into two oblongs, about nine by twelve inches. Place the two oblongs on a baking sheet that you have rinsed off with cold water. Prick them in several places with a fork. Put baking sheet in refrigerator, or some cool place, while you make the filling.

Mix cream, egg yolks, sugar, vanilla, and cornstarch together in a double boiler, and cook, stirring, over barely boiling water until custard thickens. Cool.

Bake pastry strips for ten minutes in a hot (450°) oven, then reduce heat to 350° and continue baking until pastry is brown and flaky, about twenty minutes. (Watch it, as it burns easily.) Cool, and cut each strip lengthwise into three narrow strips, trimming edges neatly.

Spread three strips with your custard. Warm the currant jelly a little so it spreads more easily, and spread this thinly on top of custard filling. Place the three plain strips of pastry on top of the three spread strips, press together lightly, dust with confectioners' sugar, and cut the lengths crosswise into separate portions about two inches wide.

Traditionally, these may be doubled in height by placing three strips, one on top of the other, with two layers of filling in between strips, but I prefer the smaller pastry.

A substitute filling can be made of whipped cream and crushed strawberries.

Mazarin Cakes (Mazariner)

1 recipe flan or tart pastry (opposite page)	⅔ cup confectioners' sugar
⅔ cup blanched almonds	1 egg (large)
¼ cup plus 1 tablespoon butter	½ teaspoon almond extract
	4 teaspoons water

Grease small tart tins well, and line them with flan or tart

dough. Grind the blanched almonds fine. Cream butter and
sugar together until smooth, and add the slightly beaten egg
and the almond extract. Add the ground almonds and continue
stirring until all ingredients are well blended.

Put filling into each pastry-lined tin, and place the filled tins
on a cooky or baking sheet. Bake about twenty minutes in a
400° oven. When tartlets are thoroughly cool, turn them out
of the tins carefully, and frost with a thin layer of icing made
from sugar and water stirred to a smooth paste.

If there is difficulty in getting baked tartlet out of tin, knock
the bottom or the edge of the little tin gently against the table
to loosen it.

Flan or Tart Pastry

⅓ cup butter, softened	1 egg
¼ cup sugar	½ teaspoon grated lemon rind
pinch of salt	1 cup flour

Mix butter, sugar, salt, egg, and lemon rind together until well
blended. Work in the flour and a very little cold water if
necessary to make a firm dough. Wrap it in wax paper, and
chill it at least an hour before using.

Half-Moon Cakes

1 recipe flan or tart pastry (see preceding recipe)
1 cup raspberry, currant, or any tartly flavored jelly
1 egg yolk mixed with 1 tablespoon cream
confectioners' sugar

Roll pastry out thin, and cut into circles with cutter slightly
smaller than a teacup. (If you haven't got a cooky cutter that

size, use a cup or a glass to cut it out with.) Place a spoonful of jelly on half of the pastry circle. Brush the edges of circle with egg yolk. Fold pastry over jelly, pressing the edges together with the tines of a fork. Brush top of pastry lightly with egg yolk.

Bake on a greased cooky sheet in a 400° oven until light brown. Sprinkle lightly with powdered sugar.

Rosettes

These cookies are so light and crisp and deliciously crunchy that although the recipe says, "will keep for months if kept in a closed tin," I find that in my house they disappear as fast as they are cool and sugared!

You need a rosette or patty mold for these.

2 eggs	1 cup flour
1 teaspoon sugar	lard, or Crisco for deep frying
pinch of salt	confectioners' sugar (in a shaker
½ teaspoon cardamom (optional)	for sprinkling)
1 cup milk	

Beat the eggs slightly with sugar, salt, and cardamom. Add milk and flour alternately, a little at a time, beating until smooth. Heat fat for frying in a deep pot. (It doesn't have to be a very large pot, as you fry the rosettes one at a time.) Heat iron a minute in hot fat, and hold it above the pot for a second to let the fat drip off. Dip it into the batter, which will cling to the iron, being careful not to cover top of iron with batter. Return to hot fat, thoroughly covering the mold, and heat for twenty to thirty-five seconds (I count slowly to thirty or thirty-five), until rosette is brown but not burned. It will slip off easily onto brown paper to drain, when it is cooked. If it

doesn't, return to hot fat for a few seconds longer. The timing
becomes very easy after the first two or three tries. And the
batter goes a long, long way. When slightly cooled, sprinkle
with confectioners' sugar.

Ginger Wafers

¾ cup butter	2 tablespoons finely ground
¾ cup sugar	black walnuts
½ cup molasses	1½ cups all-purpose flour
2 level teaspoons powdered ginger	

Melt the butter, add sugar, and stir in saucepan over low heat.
Add molasses, ginger, ground black walnuts, and lastly the
flour, adding a little at a time and stirring well to blend. Drop
by teaspoonfuls onto a greased and floured cooky sheet and
bake in a 325° oven for ten to twelve minutes. Remove from
cooky sheet immediately with a spatula, and hang cookies in-
dividually over a long-handled wooden spoon, or a wooden
dowel, supported on two coffee tins, so that they harden in a
folded shape. They are very thin and crisp. Store in a tin box.

Thinnest of Thin Almond Cookies

⅔ cup blanched almonds	1 tablespoon flour
7 tablespoons butter	2 tablespoons milk
⅓ cup plus 1 tablespoon sugar	

Grind the almonds fine, but set a few apart. In a pot, put the
ground almonds, butter, sugar, flour, and milk. Heat over a
low flame, and stir continuously until the butter has melted.
Remove immediately, and put small spoonfuls of the mixture

on well-greased and floured cooky sheets. Space them well apart, as they spread a lot. Chop coarsely the almonds you set apart, and sprinkle a few pieces on the top of each little mound of dough. Bake in 350° oven, eight to ten minutes.

When the cookies are baked, let them cool a minute on the pan, then remove them with a thin knife, and hang them immediately over a spoon as in the preceding recipe. They will shape themselves, and stiffen, looking rather like an open clamshell. These are crisp cookies and should be stored in a closed tin. Do not make them on a damp foggy day!

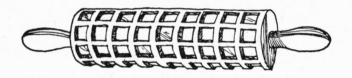

Anna's Quick Cookies

Another recipe for thin, crisp cookies.

½ stick butter	1 teaspoon vanilla
½ cup sugar	pinch of salt
1 egg	1 cup slivered almonds
3 level tablespoons flour	

Mix the softened butter together with all the other ingredients except the almonds. Place small spoonfuls two inches apart, on greased and floured cooky sheet. Pile as many slivered almonds as possible on each cooky, and bake about ten minutes in 400° oven. Wait half a minute before removing from cooky sheet with spatula.

Peach Meringue Cake

1 large meringue	½ cup peach liqueur
4 ripe peaches	1 cup heavy cream
¼ cup brandy	2 tablespoons sugar

Bake a large round meringue, dinner-plate size, and also a ring of meringue the same size around, but about two inches wide, according to meringue recipe on page 174. Peel and slice four ripe peaches, and soak for one hour in one-quarter cup brandy mixed with one-half cup peach liqueur. Turn the peach slices frequently in the liqueur.

Whip the heavy cream until stiff, adding the granulated sugar. Drain peaches well, and reserve the liqueur and juice.

Mix the peaches with the whipped cream. Split the large meringue horizontally, place bottom part on serving plate, put the open meringue ring on top of this, and fill meringue-cake with peach and whipped cream mixture. Now place top piece of meringue on this, and pour over the whole the reserved liqueur and peach juice. Cut into pie-shaped segments and serve.

Paradisnes Recipes

Gâteau St. Honoré

1 tart pastry (see page 231)   1 Pâte à Choux (see page 228)

Roll out tart dough about one-quarter inch thick, and cut it
into a circle nine inches in diameter. Prick little holes in it
with a fork. Take a pastry bag, fitted with a plain tube, and
form an edge of Pâte à Choux about three quarters of an inch
thick around the edge of the tart circle. Brush the top of the
Pâte à Choux with a little egg yolk and cream mixed. Bake in
a 425° oven for ten minutes, then reduce temperature to 325°

and bake for another twenty to thirty minutes, until edge is golden brown and looks dry. Also make about a dozen separate small puffs.

When cool, make a slit in the puffs and fill with whipped, flavored cream, or a custard. Make a thick caramel syrup by boiling one-third cup water with one cup granulated sugar, until a deep amber color. Dip bottom of filled puffs into syrup and place on top of puff ring. Fill the center of the ring with flavored whipped cream, or fruit and whipped cream mixed together. A very good filling is made by mixing one and one-half cups whipped cream with one cup raspberry jelly. Decorate with fresh or frozen berries.

Also good when puffs are filled with whipped cream and center with ice cream. Caramel sauce may be served separately with this.

Caramel Sauce

1 cup sugar   ½ teaspoon vanilla
½ cup cream

Melt the sugar in a heavy saucepan over very low heat. Heat the cream separately, then add it to the sugar very slowly, stirring all the while until it is smooth. Remove from the fire and add the vanilla.

Pâté-Aspic Hors d'Oeuvres

pâté from ½ pound chicken livers   ¼ cup Dubonnet
¾ cup bouillon   1 teaspoon gelatin

Make an aspic by beating three-quarters cup bouillon and adding to it the gelatin dissolved in the Dubonnet. Put a little liquid aspic into the bottom of tiny molds, and chill till stiff. When stiffened, put a dab of pâté on the aspic, in the center of the mold. Pour more of the slightly chilled aspic over, to fill up the mold, and chill till it is all firmly jelled. Unmold, and place each little aspic on a toast round, or a cracker. A dab of mayonnaise underneath will hold it in place on the toast.

Curried Chicken Balls (Hors d'Oeuvres)

1 broiler, or small chicken, boiled	2 eggs
	¼ cup butter
2 tablespoons chopped celery	1 tablespoon curry powder
2 teaspoons chives	salt and pepper to taste
1 teaspoon chopped parsley	bread crumbs

Take all the meat off the bones of the chicken after boiling and grind it fine, along with the celery, chives, and parsley. Mix together one of the eggs, the softened butter, the curry powder, and salt and pepper. Add this to the chicken mix. Form into small balls, roll in fine bread crumbs, then into beaten egg, and into bread crumbs again. Let chill in icebox for at least two hours. Fry in deep fat, stick a toothpick into each one, and serve with drinks.

They can be fried in advance, then reheated on a baking sheet in the oven before serving.

Délices d'Emmental

4 tablespoons butter	½ pound grated Emmentaler
5 tablespoons flour	(Swiss) cheese
1 cup milk	3 eggs, separated
⅓ cup cream	salt and pepper
	cracker meal

Melt butter in a saucepan, blend in the flour, and gradually add the milk and cream, stirring all over a low fire until smooth and thick. Stir in the cheese, take off fire and cool slightly, and stir in the three egg yolks, and salt and pepper to taste. Pour the mixture into a well-buttered shallow pan or dish about six by nine inches, and chill in refrigerator. When cold and stiff, immerse pan for a quick moment in hot water, being careful not to let water get on your cheese-paste contents. Turn the mixture out onto a board or the table. Cut it with a knife into small croquette-shaped pieces, or little squares.

Roll them in the beaten egg whites, and in cracker meal, and fry quickly in hot fat. Stick a toothpick into each one, and serve for hors d'oeuvres, or serve as a first course with tomato sauce (page 212) poured over.

Hors d'Oeuvres Anna

bread, toasted
¾ cup grated American (Cheddar, or "store") cheese
¼ cup grated Parmesan or Romano cheese
⅓ cup fresh green pepper, ground
2 eggs, separated
pinch of salt

Cut squares or rounds from toast slices, and set aside for bases. Mix together the grated cheeses, the ground green pepper, and the egg yolks. Spread on the toast rounds, or squares. Whip the egg whites stiff but not dry, with a pinch of salt. Cover the cheese mix with the whites, like a little meringue. Put on a cooky sheet and bake in a 400° oven for six to eight minutes, or until egg white begins to take on a little color. Serve immediately while hot.

Rolled Cheese Ball

1 3-ounce package cream cheese	1 tablespoon finely chopped parsley
8 ounces Gorgonzola, or any blue cheese	1 cup finely chopped walnuts
¼ cup heavy cream	dash of Worcestershire sauce

Mix the cheeses, cream, parsley, and Worcestershire sauce together, blending well until smooth and creamy. Chill until quite firm. Roll the cheese mixture into a ball and when shaped roll it in the chopped nuts until it is well covered all over.

Keep it chilled until it is to be used, and serve as a spread with crackers.

Caviar Roulade

4 tablespoons butter	2 cups milk
½ cup flour	4 eggs, separated

Preheat the oven to 325° and grease a ten-by-fifteen-inch jelly roll pan, or a cooky sheet with edges. Line the pan with wax paper, a little longer than the pan so that you can grab hold of it later, to remove the contents. Grease, and sprinkle the wax paper with flour.

Melt the butter, blend in the flour, add the milk, and continue stirring over low heat until the mixture bubbles and is nice and smooth. Remove it from the heat and add the slightly beaten egg yolks, stirring well. Beat the egg whites stiff and fold into mixture. Spread this in your prepared pan, and bake it on lower rack of oven for about forty minutes, or until the top is a rich golden brown and rebounds to the touch when you poke it with your finger. Turn it out onto wax paper, removing any of the paper that clings to the top side.

Filling

> 8 ounces pressed black caviar   4 ounces cream cheese
> 1 cup sour cream

Put the pressed caviar into a bowl, add the sour cream, and mush them together with a fork. The pressed caviar will seem very stiff and gluey at first, but persevere and you will see a miracle take place. The caviar will gradually absorb the sour cream and expand until (at one half the price!) it looks and tastes like the real, big plump grains of fresh Beluga caviar.

Reserve half of this mixture for the outside of your roulade, and mix the other half with the cream cheese, to fill the roulade. Spread this filling evenly over the cooled roulade, and roll the whole thing up like a jelly roll, with the help of the underneath piece of wax paper, and transfer it to a platter. Now spread the rest of the caviar–sour cream mixture on top of the rolled-up roulade, and garnish with a little chopped chives, or scallion tops, finely cut.

To serve, cut slantwise in one-and-one-half-inch slices, and hear your guests ooh and ah! Serves ten.

Red Caviar Dip

4 ounces cream cheese	4-ounce jar of red caviar (salmon roe)
1 tablespoon sour cream	
¼ teaspoon lemon juice	1 tablespoon finely chopped chives or scallion tops

Blend the cream cheese, sour cream, lemon juice, and caviar together, mushing it with a fork. Add the chopped chives or scallion tops, mixing all together well. Chill for at least two hours before serving. When it is first made it is fairly runny, but will stiffen up again in refrigerator. It may be used as a dip, or spread on crackers. If you wish to spread it on crackers, do it while you are having your drinks. The crackers get soggy if done ahead of time.

Tante Kirsten's Ham and Foie Gras Entrée

6 rounds of toasted bread, 3 inches in diameter	6 small slices of ham (same size)
6 artichoke bottoms	6 slices of Pâté de Foie Gras, about ¼-inch thick

Place the toasted bread rounds on six individual plates that you are going to serve them on. Warm the artichoke bottoms and the ham, slightly, in a little stock. Place the artichoke bottoms on the toast rounds, then a slice of ham, cut to fit, on each artichoke. On top of this place a slice of foie gras, also cut to fit, and pour over the whole the Madeira Sauce.

Madeira Sauce

1 cup clear brown stock	1 teaspoon potato flour
¼ cup Madeira	3 teaspoons chopped truffles

Take the clear brown stock, or bouillon, to which you have
added the Madeira, and bring to a boil. Add a teaspoon of
potato flour, stirred out in one-quarter cup cold water, and the
chopped truffles. Bring to a boil again and let cool one minute,
while stirring. Serve.

Pâté Maison (Leverpostej)

2 tablespoons chopped shallots	½ teaspoon dried tarragon
4 tablespoons butter	2 tablespoons heavy cream
½ pound chicken livers	salt and freshly ground pepper
3 tablespoons brandy (warmed)	to taste

Cook chopped shallots in 1 tablespoon butter until soft. Remove shallots from pan and reserve. Add remaining butter to
pan and sauté the chicken livers over a quick fire for four or
five minutes. Do not overcook. Pour warm brandy over livers
and ignite. Remove pan from heat and add shallots, cream, tarragon, salt and pepper.

Pour mixture (in small quantities) into a blender and blend
until smooth. Pour mixture into a bowl and chill for at least
four hours before serving.

This pâté, because of the preserving quality of the brandy,
keeps well in the refrigerator for ten days.

Blender Borscht

3 to 4 beets	1 cup sour cream
½ cup cabbage, shredded	dill weed
3 cups beef stock, or consommé	salt and pepper to taste

Boil the beets until tender, peel, and cut in quarters. Steam the
shredded cabbage for five minutes. Place vegetables in blender,

a little at a time, with part of stock. (Always blend in small quantities. The blender should never be more than one-third full at the most.) When vegetables are puréed, put in a saucepan, add any stock not used, season with salt and pepper, and bring to a boil.

Serve hot, with a spoonful of sour cream in each cup and a sprinkling of chopped dill. May also be served cold. In this case you may want to thin the soup with a little more stock or bouillon. Thin slices of dark rye bread, or Russian pumpernickel, spread with sweet butter, go well with this.

Lina's Cheese Snaps (Lina's Ostekjeks)

1 cup butter	1 cup flour
¾ cup grated Emmentaler or Gruyère cheese	2 eggs
¼ cup grated Parmesan cheese	¼ teaspoon Worcestershire sauce
	seasoned salt or caraway seeds

Place softened butter and grated cheeses in a bowl and stir well until blended. Add flour, 1 egg, and Worcestershire sauce, continuing to mix all well together. Let dough stand in a cool place to become firm enough to shape into a roll about two and one-half inches in diameter. Sprinkle a piece of wax paper either with seasoned salt, or caraway seeds, according to taste, and roll the cheese roll in this until it is lightly coated all over.

Roll up the cheese roll in the wax paper and refrigerate until hard enough to cut into quarter-inch slices. Place on a cooky sheet, brush the tops with slightly beaten egg, and bake in a

400° oven eight to ten minutes, or until just beginning to
brown at the edges. I use these plain for cocktails, but sometimes make them a little larger, and with a filling serve them
as a first course.

Filling

Combine one-half cup butter and one-quarter cup grated
Parmesan cheese. Add a few drops of Worcestershire sauce
and stir all well together. When the cheese snaps have cooled,
stick two together like a sandwich, with the filling in between.

Breast of Chicken, Asparagus

1 carrot	1 cup chicken broth
1 small onion	¼ cup dry vermouth
2 stalks celery	1 tablespoon brandy
4 chicken breasts (single)	1 cup heavy cream
1 teaspoon dried or chopped	1 can white asparagus
fresh tarragon	salt and pepper to taste

Chop carrot, onion, and celery fine, and put in the bottom of
a casserole. Place the chicken breasts on the chopped vegetables, add the tarragon, chicken broth, vermouth, and brandy.
Put lid on casserole and cook in a 350° oven for forty-five
minutes. Strain off all liquid from the casserole into a smaller
saucepan (leaving chicken in the casserole with lid on, but
off the fire). Reduce liquid in saucepan by half.

Drain, and heat the asparagus in a double boiler, while the
sauce is reducing. Add cream to sauce, bring to a boil and
cook for five minutes, adding salt and pepper to taste. Place
the asparagus around the chicken in the casserole, and pour
hot sauce over all. Garnish with a little chopped parsley.

Pink Sauce

½ cup cream, whipped stiff	a few drops of lemon juice
½ cup mayonnaise	3 tablespoons tomato ketchup
½ teaspoon grated onion	

Fold the whipped cream into the mayonnaise. Add the grated onion, lemon juice, and ketchup to this, and stir all together until well blended. Serve in a separate bowl, to accompany grilled or fried fish.

Fish Mousse (Fiskepudding)

3 pounds haddock or cod (or 1½ pounds flounder fillets)	2 teaspoons salt
	a small pinch of Nepal pepper
1½ cups light cream	½ teaspoon grated nutmeg
½ cup milk	bread crumbs
4 tablespoons potato starch	

If it is a whole piece of fish, remove all the skin and bones. Mince the raw fish in small quantities at a time in the blender, adding gradually the cream, milk, potato starch, and salt and pepper. The whole mass should be ground three times.

Fill a buttered, bread-crumbed mold about three-quarters full with the fish mixture. Place mold in a pan with at least an inch of water in it, and bake in a 350° oven for one and one-quarter hours. If the top becomes too brown, put a piece of foil over it.

When cooked, invert the mold carefully onto a platter, and pour over the fish mousse a cream sauce with either lobster pieces or shrimp added, and a little sherry. Garnish with chopped dill or parsley.

Fillets of Fish à la Mode de Chez Nous

4 good-sized fillets of flounder
 or sole
1 tablespoon chopped shallots
1 cup white wine
1 dozen scallops
1 dozen large shrimps, boiled
 and peeled

1 dozen small oysters
1 teaspoon chopped tarragon
1 cup thick cream sauce
salt and Nepal pepper
 to taste

This is a lovely dish, and can be made ahead of time and re-heated. I use for it whatever shellfish is available at the time, and if I am making it in my house on the coast of Maine, I go down to the rocky beach and gather mussels for it, or persuade my sons to dig me some clams.

Simmer the fillets of fish and the chopped shallots gently in the white wine for five minutes. (I find it easiest to handle them in a large frying pan.) Lift the fillets out carefully with a wide spatula, letting the wine drain off them back into the pan, and place them in a buttered baking dish. If the scallops are large, cut them in quarters. Save three or four of the shrimps for garnishing, and place the rest of the shrimps, scallops, and oysters in the baking dish with the fish.

Add the tarragon to the wine, and reduce the wine by boiling to half its quantity. Make a thick cream sauce according to the recipe on page 172, and add the reduced wine to this. Season with salt and pepper and pour the sauce over the fish and shellfish in the baking dish. Bake in a preheated 350° oven for twenty to twenty-five minutes.

Garnish with the extra shrimps, and a little chopped dill or parsley. If you want to be really fancy, pipe mashed potatoes around the edge of your dish, before setting in oven to bake.

Fillets of Fish with Crab Meat

This is made in the same way as the preceding recipe, substituting one pint of crab meat for the shellfish, and adding one tablespoon of sherry to the sauce. The crab meat and sauce are spread in a layer over the cooked fillets of fish and dotted with butter before being put in the oven.

Mock Turtle Stew (Forloren Skilpadde)

A very elegant party dish, nothing like our mock turtle soup. This is an elaborate dish, and I suggest that you start preparing it the day before you are planning to serve it.

1 pound fish fillets, flounder or haddock	½ teaspoon grated nutmeg
2 tablespoons butter	5 tablespoons ordinary flour, or potato starch
2 eggs	3 cups thin cream, or whole milk
1½ teaspoons salt	
very small pinch of Nepal pepper or slightly more white pepper	

Be sure all the bones have been removed from the fish fillets, and grind fish fine three times. Add the softened butter, the eggs, one at a time, and the seasoning, mixing it all in well. Add the flour and the milk alternately to the fish mixture, stirring and finally kneading it well, after each addition. If it seems too thick, add a little more milk, but remember it is going to be formed into balls, and poached. If it doesn't seem thick enough to hold its shape, add a little more flour. Form into small balls, and poach gently in salted water for ten minutes. Set aside. Now make some small meatballs of the same size.

1 pound veal	1 pound veal stew meat (optional)
¼ pound fresh pork	tongue (whole)
1 egg	3 eggs, hard-boiled
½ cup cream	butter for browning
½ cup fine bread crumbs	1 pound mushrooms
salt and pepper	

Grind together one pound of veal and the fresh pork. Grind three times. (Or, if you are on good terms with your butcher, have him do it.) Beat egg and cream together slightly. Mix this into the meat, alternately with the bread crumbs. Add salt and pepper to taste. Form into small balls and brown in a little butter until done. (About ten minutes.) We also sometimes added one pound of veal stew, cut into small pieces and cooked until tender, to "stretch" the dish. Set aside.

Boil a whole tongue until done, according to size. When cooled, remove skin and cut slices about one-half inch thick, and cut these up into small cubes, so that you have about one and one-half cups. Wash and slice mushrooms, dry well, and cook in a little butter for about ten minutes. Now you can relax until tomorrow!

Sauce

1½ tablespoons butter	salt and pepper to taste
2 tablespoons flour	½ cup Madeira
1½ cups beef stock or bouillon	2 tablespoons brandy
1 tablespoon tomato purée	

Melt the butter, stir in the flour, and gradually add the bouillon or stock, stirring over a low flame until it thickens. Stir in the tomato purée and the remaining ingredients. Put into this the meatballs (twelve to fifteen), fish balls (twelve to fifteen), and tongue. Bring to a boil, heat gently for five minutes, take off the fire and serve, garnished with the hard-boiled eggs cut into sixths, and a little chopped parsley. Really worth all that effort!

All this may seem like a great expenditure of time for one dish, but it is an unusually good one when made correctly, and also, you have all sorts of fringe benefits from the leftover ingredients that you have prepared. You can make several different dishes all the rest of the week, with very little effort. Or you can freeze both meatballs and fish balls left over. The leftover fish balls can be served in a thin cream sauce, the meatballs in a variety of ways, and the tongue is delicious, sliced and reheated with a purée of spinach.

Now, if the dish intrigues you, but you have neither the time nor the inclination to put in all those hours on it, here is a very short shortcut.

Buy a tin of Norwegian fish balls, drain them well, and since they are quite large, cut them into thirds. Buy a tin of small (cocktail size) meatballs. Buy a little glass jar of tongue and cut it up into small cubes. Hard-boil the eggs, and proceed to make the sauce as directed. It will not have the full flavor of the other, but still makes a "different" dish.

Ptarmigan (Ryper)

ptarmigan	3/4 cup sour cream
salt and pepper	1 teaspoon flour
butter	several slices goat cheese
1 cup stock	

When the birds have been plucked, rinse them off, dry them well, and rub a little salt and pepper into them. Put a little butter into an iron pot (Dutch oven) and sear them on all sides. Add one cup of stock (made from necks and giblets, or bouillon) and let birds simmer in this, with the lid on, for one hour, basting them frequently. Add three-quarters cup sour cream with one teaspoon flour stirred out in it to the stock. Add several slices of Norwegian goat cheese (Gjetost) stirred into the sauce, to heighten the flavor. Serve the birds with some of the sauce poured over, and the rest served separately. A tart jelly, or lingonberry jam, goes well with this.

Corned Brisket of Beef (Sprengt Oksebryst)

3 to 4 pounds corned brisket of beef	1 white turnip, peeled and cut up
1 teaspoon coarsely ground pepper	1 bay leaf
	3 or 4 cloves
	a few pieces of celery tops

If meat is very salty, soak it for eight to ten hours, changing the water once or twice. Remove the bones, dry the meat well, and sprinkle pepper over one side of it. Then roll the meat up, and tie securely with string. Place in a pot with enough cold water to cover it. Add the turnip, bay leaf, cloves, and celery tops to the pot. Bring to a boil, remove scum as it forms on surface, and simmer meat, covered, for three or four hours, or until tender.

Serve with boiled potatoes, boiled cabbage, carrots, and peas. A thin cream sauce (page 172), with horseradish added to it, may be served as acompaniment.

Overturned Apple Cake

1 cup sugar	5 or 6 apples
¼ cup water	1 teaspoon cinnamon
1 teaspoon butter	tart pastry (see page 231)

Caramelize sugar and water by cooking in a pan until it is a dark amber color, then pour it into the bottom of a well-buttered pie or tart tin. Peel, core, and cut the apples into thin slices. Place them, slightly overlapping, on the caramelized sugar in the pie tin and dot with butter. Sprinkle cinnamon over the apple slices. Cover fruit completely with a circle of tart pastry, and bake the whole thing in a 400° oven until crust is light brown. (Twenty-five to thirty minutes.) Remove from oven. Cover tart with a plate, slightly larger than the pie tin, and on which you will serve it. Reverse the tart quickly onto the plate, being sure to get all the sugary goo out of the bottom of the pan. The pastry will be on the bottom, and the caramel-glazed fruit on the top.

Pots de Crème, Mocha-Chocolate

2 cups medium cream	4 ounces semi-sweet chocolate
½ cup strong black coffee	7 egg yolks

Heat the cream but do not boil. Put the coffee in a saucepan and melt the chocolate in it over a low flame. When melted, add it to the hot cream. Beat the egg yolks in a bowl and slowly pour the hot cream mixture over them, stirring all the while. If not absolutely smooth, strain through a sieve and pour the custard into small, individual custard cups. Set them in a pan with an inch or two of hot water (a roasting pan does very well for this), cover with a piece of foil, and bake in a 300° oven for twenty to twenty-five minutes. Chill thoroughly and serve. A crisp cooky (pages 232 to 234) goes well with this.

Consommé Double au Madère

At Paradisnes soup stock was made often by Lina-cook, who almost always had a large pot simmering gently on the back of the coal stove, and into this she put all the scraps and trimmings of meat from her roasts, and any extra leftover vegetables. This was used for sauces and soups. But for a special "party" consommé, she started from scratch.

3 or 4 pounds of shank or shin of beef	a few stalks of celery
1 pound beef, chuck or round	1 teaspoon whole white peppercorns
1 carrot	2 quarts cold water
2 leeks	

Put all ingredients into a large pot, cover with water, and bring slowly to a boil. Skim off the scum that forms on the surface. Cover pot with a lid and let simmer gently for several hours. Cook until meat falls apart, and you have extracted all the flavor from it. Strain the stock, discarding meat, bones, and vegetables. (Give them when cool to the dog. He'll still get some good out of them.) Let stock cool, and skim off all fat from the surface.

To clear: Heat the stock and whisk into it three egg whites. Let it boil for five minutes, then remove from the heat, and let stand for fifteen minutes. Strain it through a muslin cloth, wrung out in cold water, or through five or six thicknesses of cheesecloth. Strain twice, or until completely clear. Salt to taste. Serve with a teaspoon of Madeira to each cup.

Filets de Sole, Bonne Maman (Mormor's Fin-Fin Fiske File)

4 tablespoons butter
1 tablespoon finely chopped shallots
½ pound mushrooms, sliced
1 tablespoon chopped parsley
6 fillets of sole or small fillets of flounder
3 ripe tomatoes, peeled, seeded, and chopped coarsely
½ teaspoon salt
a small dash of Nepal pepper
1 cup dry white wine
2 tablespoons cream sauce (page 172)
½ teaspoon tomato paste
2 tablespoons whipped cream

Put two tablespoons butter in a flat saucepan and add the shallots, mushrooms, half the parsley, and the fish fillets. Put the chopped tomatoes on top, the rest of the parsley, and season with salt and Nepal pepper. Add the white wine (and a little fish stock, if you have any at hand). Cover saucepan with a piece of wax paper, bring to a boil, then turn flame down and let simmer slowly for ten to twelve minutes, depending on the thickness of the fish. Remove the fillets carefully to a heat-proof serving dish, draining juice from them back into the pan, and cook the liquid until reduced to one third of its original quantity. Add cream sauce to thicken, and tomato paste, and gradually, bit by bit, the remaining butter. Taste for seasoning. Just before serving add the whipped cream to the sauce, pour it over the fillets, and glaze for a minute under the broiler.

The whipped cream helps to give a golden brown color, but to do this the broiler must be very hot.

Filet de Boeuf, Écossais

Two filets of the very best Scottish beef were procured for this dinner. Scottish beef is *almost* as good as American! The two filets were simply covered by thin slices of larding pork, to keep them from drying out, and were roasted in a 400° oven; one of them for twenty-five minutes, for those who liked their meat rare, the other for about eight minutes longer. Small potato balls, browned in butter, were served with this. Also, a platter of tiny fresh vegetables accompanied by Rørt Smør (Lemon Butter, page 257).

Vegetables Printanière

In Paris, in the spring, the vegetable stalls have signs on them announcing "Les Primeurs" — the first, the earliest vegetables up from the South. Bunches of fingerling carrots, nestling in crisp green parsley; white-tipped rosy radishes, hot to the tongue; the first fat green asparagus; tiny green peas, and beautiful creamy white heads of cauliflower.

In Norway we were limited in the number of varieties, but the vegetables were all picked young and fresh. A large well-arranged platter of assorted vegetables usually accompanied a roast or a whole boiled fish.

The well-drained boiled cauliflower was placed in the center of a large platter, often with a circle of whole small baked tomatoes around it. Radiating, as from the sun, were little new potatoes, tiny carrots, cooked whole, the Sukkererter (Mange-Tout or Snow-Peas) in their pods, and, a little later, slender string beans, picked when young and tender.

The vegetables were served with either a Hollandaise Sauce, or with Rørt Smør (Lemon Butter).

Hollandaise Sauce

¼ pound butter	pinch of salt and pepper
3 egg yolks	¼ teaspoon chopped fresh or
1 teaspoon lemon juice	dried tarragon (optional)
1 tablespoon hot water	

Cut the butter into several parts, and put a third of it in the top of a double boiler over hot water, with the three egg yolks and the tablespoon of hot water. Stir mixture rapidly and continually, not quite allowing the water underneath to boil. Add the rest of the butter at intervals, continuing to stir as it melts and the sauce thickens. Add lemon juice, salt, pepper, and tarragon. Remove from the fire and beat a minute longer.

If sauce must be kept waiting a few minutes, put lid on pot, and tilt top of boiler up over lower part, so that it isn't quite touching the water, but will keep warm.

Lemon Butter (Rørt Smør)

¼ pound butter	¼ teaspoon coarsely ground
1 tablespoon lemon juice	pepper
½ teaspoon salt	

Soften the butter to room temperature. With a fork, work the lemon juice, salt, and pepper into it. Form it into a round pat and mark the top of the pat in a swirling design with the tines of the fork. Chill enough to become firm before serving as accompaniment to vegetables or fish.

Cold Duck, with Pâté

Roast one duck and let it cool. Make pâté (page 244) from one pound of chicken livers (or fresh duck livers, if you are fortunate enough to find them). Now with a sharp knife, pull the duck breast away from the backbone, making a pocket that you stuff with the pâté. Do this to both breasts. Now re-shape the plumper duck breast back into place. Decorate it down the middle of the breastbone with slices of pitted green olives, or pieces of truffle. When you carve the duck to serve it, cut one-inch slices crosswise, on a slight slant. Each piece should be partly duck and partly pâté. Serve with endive, or any other green salad.

For the Prince's Dinner, the ducks were skinned after being roasted, and when cold, covered with aspic, the whole being decorated with truffle slices cut in fancy shapes.

Poires, Son Altesse

This beautiful dessert, pure invention of the moment, was the result of Tante Kirsten's imagination and Lina-cook's culinary skill.

It had as its base a round of sponge cake on which rested a pyramid of ices, made in a mold and tricolored like the Italian flag. The lemon ice (white) in the middle was supported by raspberry ice (red) on one side, and crème de menthe flavored ice (green) on the other. Around the base of the pyramid, radiating from it, were poached pears . . . but such pears! To begin with, they were absolutely flawless, and picked for their uniformity of size. They were carefully peeled, cored, and cut in half. Then they were gently poached in a syrup made from two cups water and one cup sugar boiled together until tender (about five minutes), and at the last a little raspberry syrup was added to turn them ever so faintly pink. The stems had been cut off, and each stem replaced by a slim green one made of candied angélique (angelica). Those smooth, pink fleshy-looking pears with the little green stems standing perkily up in the air were a lovely sight to behold. In fact, Uncle Magnus started to laugh as they were passed to the Prince, and I heard him say something about "little pigs' bottoms or . . ." but Tante Kirsten gave him a stern look that stopped him.

Lina's Plain Health Soup

1 onion, chopped	2 or 3 stalks of celery
3 leeks, cleaned and cut into	a handful of Swiss chard or
1-inch segments	spinach leaves
3 tablespoons butter	a handful of rice
2 sliced carrots	salt and pepper

Cook the onion and the leeks in butter until soft. Add to this the carrots, celery, and spinach or chard leaves, cut up fine. Pour over all this two quarts of water and throw in a small handful of rice. Let boil for thirty minutes, strain through a coarse sieve, and add salt and pepper to taste. (The cooked vegetables and rice should be pushed through the strainer back into the broth.)

Very good after too much rich food!

Carrot-Rice Soup

3 carrots	4 cups chicken stock
2 stalks of celery	2 tablespoons cream
½ small onion, chopped fine	salt to taste
½ cup rice	

Cut up the carrots and celery, add the chopped onion, and boil in water just to cover, until tender. (Save this water and add it to your stock.) Boil the rice until soft, and add it to your chicken stock.

Purée the cooked vegetables through a food mill, or coarse strainer, directly into the stock and rice. Add cream and bring to a boil. Add salt to taste. Serve with thin Ry-Krisp, or even thinner Flatbrød.

Index

Index

Veal
  and Beef Sausage, *112*
  Chops in Casserole, *119*, 225–226
  Kidneys, Swiss Style, *111–112*, 222
  Orloff, *103*, 213–214
  Paprikash, *49–50*, *94–95*, 187–188
  Patties, *45–46*, 184
  Roast, *147*
  Sautéed, *91*, 199–200
  Spiced, 6, *111*
  Sweetbreads with Ham, Mushrooms in Sherry Sauce, *111*, 221
  Thin Fillets of, Norwegian Style, *91*, 199–200
Vegetables, *20–21*, *110*

Vegetables (*contd.*)
  Cauliflower with Shrimps, *21*, 171–172
  and Fish Chowder, *29*, 179–180
  Printanière, 256–257
  Snow Peas, *20*, 171, 257
  Velvet Pudding, *91*, 200
  Verte, Sauce, *53*, 190

  Wafer Shells, *17*, 167–168
  Waffles, *45*, *58*
  Norwegian Style, 183
  Wild Strawberry Jam, *45*, 183–184
  Wine Aspic, *137*

  Yellow Pea Soup, 71, 192

82191